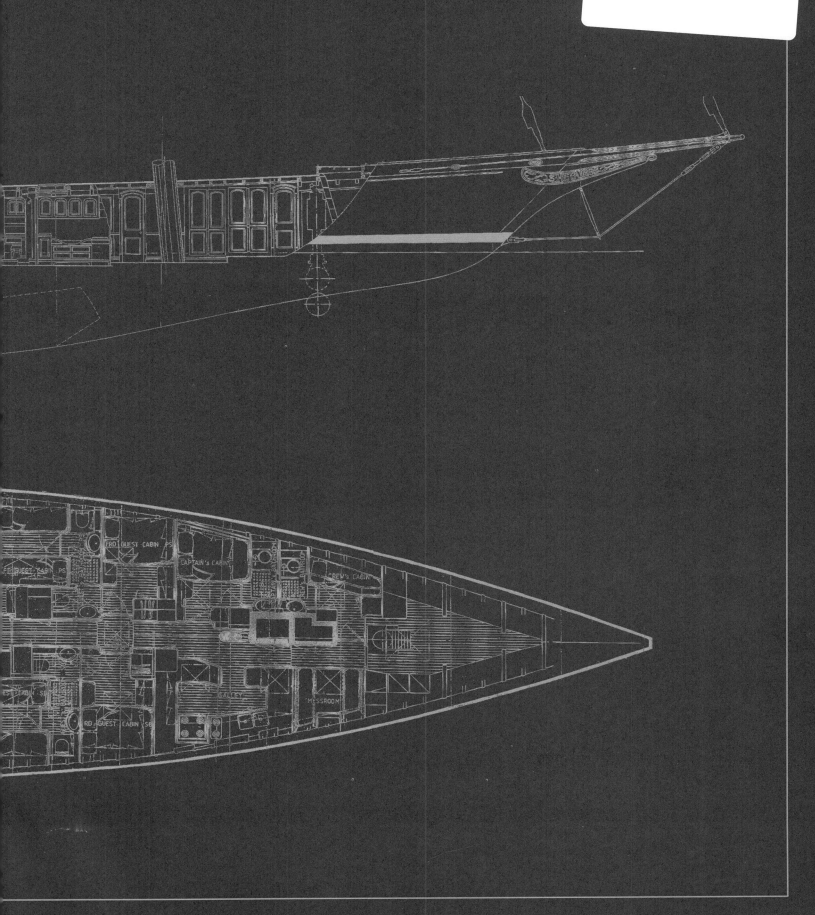

SuperYachts

Super Yachts

AN ILLUSTRATED TOUR OF SOME OF
THE WORLD'S MOST LUXURIOUS YACHTS

TEXT BY JOHN JULIAN

PHOTOGRAPHS BY MICHAEL NG AND PAUL TODD

Hodder Moa Beckett

Acknowledgements

All photographs by Michael Ng and Paul Todd, except the following:

Front cover and title page
Ivor Wilkins, courtesy of Alloy Yachts International Ltd

Inside front flap
Liberty, courtesy of Perini Navi SpA

Itasca
Pages 34, 38-39 — Newport Yacht Services Inc.
Pages 36, 37, 40 — Julie Plummer and Max Cumming

Andromeda la Dea
Pages 51, 52 — Perini Navi SpA

Double Haven
Pages 56-62 — M.Y. *Double Haven*

Yanneke Too
Pages 73, 74, 76 (top) — SY *Yanneke Too*

Sapphire
Pages 82-83 — Holland Jachtbouw BV

Charlatan
Pages 93, 99 — Ivor Wilkins, courtesy of Alloy Yachts International Ltd
Pages 94, 97 — Martin Fine, courtesy of Alloy Yachts International Ltd

Liberty
Pages 103, 104-105, 106-107 — Perini Navi SpA

Freesia
Page 108 — Terry Fong, AFA Photography

Independence
Pages 117, 118 — Perini Navi SpA

Spada
Page 122 — Terry Fong, AFA Photography

Affinity
Pages 132-133 (details) — Martin Fine, courtesy of Delta Marine Industries

Georgia
Pages 137, 142-143 — Ivor Wilkins, courtesy of Alloy Yachts International Ltd
Pages 138-139, 140-141, 142-143 — Martin Fine, courtesy of Alloy Yachts International Ltd

ISBN 1-86958-819-3

© 2000 Original text — John Julian
© 2000 Photographs — Michael Ng and Paul Todd
The moral rights of the authors have been asserted.

© 2000 — Design and format Hodder Moa Beckett Publishers Ltd

Published in 2000 by Hodder Moa Beckett Publishers Ltd
[a member of the Hodder Headline Group],
4 Whetu Place, Mairangi Bay, Auckland, New Zealand

Designed and produced by Hodder Moa Beckett Publishers Ltd
Colour separations by Microdot, Auckland
Printed by Toppan Printing Co., Hong Kong

For Molly Julian

Contents

Introduction

The early 1930s saw the last high-water mark for big yachts in more than half a century. The mighty 'J' Class cutters were competing for the America's Cup, and the last of the great steam yachts, *Nahlin* and *Corsair IV*, had just been built for British and American owners respectively. Memories of the Depression and the Great War were slowly receding, and the threat of further conflict was not yet fully apparent. But vast social changes in the wake of the Second World War put paid to yachting at this level for many years. The industry would continue, but on a diminished scale.

There are many reasons for the recent renaissance of the great yachts, including modern machinery and materials as well as space-age navigation and communications systems. New vessels have been built and older ones restored. Grand yachting has always been the preserve of the affluent, and what was once the exclusive domain of royalty and nobility also became the pastime of the very rich. It makes fascinating history.

The word 'yacht' is rooted in the Dutch language of the 16th century. King Philip II of Spain ruled the Netherlands at the time, and he was not popular. The Dutch developed a fast sailing warship called a jaght, from the word for hunt, or chase. Many of these were built to fight the Spaniards in the rivers and canals of the Netherlands, and, when the Dutch won their independence, the jaghts were developed for commercial use as the country became Europe's leading maritime nation. Some were built for private purposes as well and by the middle of the 17th century yachting and yacht racing were well under way around Holland.

Perhaps you have been to the pyramids at Giza and seen the 40 m barge built for Cheops. This dates from 2600 BC, and while it may not have been built expressly for fun, it wasn't a trading vessel either. Cleopatra had a barge as well, and the Romans are thought to have sailed for enjoyment on Lake Nemi. Back in northern Europe, the kings of Norway, Denmark and England owned vessels for pleasure in the 10th and 11th centuries. But the sport of yachting did not really take hold until the Restoration of Charles II in England, during 1660, when the Dutch East India Company gave him a yacht called *Mary*. A year later, the King raced his brother, the Duke of York, from Greenwich to Gravesend and back. The Duke's yacht won the outward leg, but the King triumphed on the way home, so the stake of £100 was evenly divided.

Yachting would remain the sport of kings for nearly 300 years, although others wealthy enough to share their monarch's pleasure would become owners themselves. Yacht clubs began to emerge during the course of the 18th century, the Royal Cork Yacht Club being the first to be formed in 1720 as the Water Club of Cork. The Cumberland Sailing Society, named for King George III's brother, was established on the River Thames in 1775. This association later became the Royal Thames Yacht Club. In 1815, the Yacht Club was founded, the Prince Regent joining in 1817, three years before he became King George IV. The Royal Yacht Club, as it became known upon his accession, would move to Cowes on the Isle of Wight in 1824, and assume the style of the Royal Yacht Squadron in 1833. A system of handicapping had been devised by this time, and racing was close and keen, with fleets ranging in size from small cutters to square rigged yachts of more than 300 tons.

Many more clubs would soon flourish in England, Scotland and Wales, while others would be established overseas. In 1838, the Royal Hobart Regatta Association was founded, followed in 1844 by the Royal Bermuda Yacht Club, and the Royal New Zealand Yacht Squadron in 1859. In Australia, the Royal Prince Alfred Yacht Club was founded in Sydney during 1867, the Royal South Australian Yacht Squadron in Adelaide by 1869, and the Royal Perth Yacht Club in 1875. Other clubs were started in Gibraltar, India, Canada and South Africa between 1829 and 1858. Meanwhile the New York Yacht Club had been founded in 1844, seven years before the schooner *America* arrived in Cowes to win the Hundred Guinea Trophy donated by the Marquess of Anglesey to the Royal Yacht Squadron, which would henceforth be known as the America's Cup.

Royalty would continue to lead the way for many years in the ownership of the great yachts. The Royal Yacht, which Queen Victoria inherited in 1837, was a three-masted man o' war called the *Royal George*, which had served three monarchs before her. This vessel was replaced in 1843 by the first *Victoria and Albert*, a steam yacht of 1034 tons, and 225 ft in length, which was used for the first State visit to France for more than 300 years. Her successor, *Victoria and Albert II*, built in 1855, was 2470 tons, and 300 ft long, with a complement of 240 officers and men, and would travel as far as St Petersburg in 1896 for the coronation of Tsar Nicholas II. The third yacht to bear this name was larger still at 5500 tons, and her crew of 407 would include 40 royal servants. This twin-screw steamer would serve the royal family from her commissioning in 1901 until Queen Elizabeth II's accession in 1953, although her last official appearance would take place in 1937. The 412 ft, 12,000 hp *Britannia* would take her place, but would be decommissioned during the late 1990s.

Elsewhere, Queen Victoria's grandson, Kaiser Wilhelm II of Germany, had built *Hohenzollern* in 1893. This was bigger and faster than his grandmother's *Victoria and Albert II*, being 385 ft long, and capable of 21.5 knots. But the Tsar of All the Russias had trumped them both as long before as 1880, when the Scottish yard of John Elder had built him a triple-screw steam yacht of 11,000 tons, which was 266 ft in length with an incredible 153 ft beam. This magnificent, if rather portly, vessel was subsequently kept in the Black Sea, but the luckless Alexander II was never to enjoy his new yacht, as he was assassinated before she reached Sevastopol. The purpose of this one-upmanship between the countries was two-fold: national pride, and the pursuit of maritime superiority over Great Britain.

Heads of other European nations had also come to recognise the prestige afforded by a large yacht. Napoleon III was a member of the Royal Yacht Squadron, and had a barquentine called *La Reine Hortense*. The Austro-Hungarian Emperor owned a London-built paddle yacht of 1830 tons called *Miramar*. Victor Emmanuel II of Italy had commissioned the 3266 ton screw barquentine *Savoia* in 1883, and other grand vessels were constructed for the rulers of Denmark, Portugal, Spain, Sweden and Turkey. In the meantime, successive American presidents were making do with the 1465 ton, three-masted screw schooner *Dolphin*, built during 1884 in Chester, Pennsylvania, although Taft, McKinley and Roosevelt made more use of the smaller, 152 ton *Sylph*.

While all this was going on, some non-royal owners were putting in some serious sea time. George Crowninshield's *Cleopatra's Barge*, probably the first large yacht built in America, had sailed the Atlantic and cruised the Mediterranean before returning home in October 1817. This 100 ft topsail schooner had been built in Salem by Becket's Shipyard at a reputed cost of $50,000, a substantial sum in those days, but a fraction of the fortune that Crowninshield had amassed during the War of 1812. Sixty years later Thomas (later Lord) Brassey would circumnavigate the globe with his family and 34 crew aboard his yacht *Sunbeam*. This 170 ft, composite, three-masted topsail schooner of 576 tons had two

Super yachts in Auckland's Viaduct Basin.

auxiliary steam engines which enabled her to remain at sea for up to 11 days without bunkering, and longer with a favourable wind. She would cover 35,400 nautical miles during the course of her voyage. By the time a further 60 years had elapsed *Nahlin*, the 1574 ton, steam-turbine-driven yacht belonging to the jute millionairess Lady Yule would have circled the world again, visiting New Zealand during 1934 as part of her South Pacific itinerary. Remarkably, this yacht would survive after many years spent languishing on the River Danube, and would be returned to Great Britain at the end of 1999.

By the time Edward VII, a keen sailor, had been crowned shortly after Cowes Week in 1902, yachting in Great Britain was in full swing. The Boer War was over, as was the period of mourning for Queen Victoria, and the country was at the height of its powers. Kaiser Wilhelm II was a frequent visitor with his yacht *Meteor*, and Kiel Week had emerged as the most important sailing fixture on the calendar next to Cowes. The only thing that seemed to detract from the King's enjoyment of his 122 ft racing cutter *Britannia* was his cousin's uncompromising approach to the sport, and the alarming expansion of the Imperial German Navy.

Many British businessmen, in addition to the aristocracy and landed gentry, sought to emulate the King at sea, as well as ashore. Income tax was negligible, so those with some capital could afford this indulgence, and designers and builders such as Fay, Fife, Nicholson, Storey, and Watson were keeping busy, as were their antipodean counterparts Messrs Bailey and Logan. The industry attracted talent, which, in turn, drew apprentices into the craft. Riggers, sailmakers, and professional crew, among others, were to benefit from the boom, and more modern building methods involved shipwrights with experience in composite construction. With active royal patronage, the big yachts were to survive the first 40 years of the 20th century, including the vast social upheaval of the Great War. However, the advent of increased taxation, and the paucity of crew at the end of the Second World War, spelt the end for most of these vessels. Yachts that had survived naval service would be laid up or sent to the breakers. It would take many years for the industry to recover.

There are various reasons for the resurgence of yachting, and some of them have to do with broader access to the sport at entry level. Post war dinghy sailors went on to compete in offshore racing, which enjoyed a revival during the 1950s. Many would participate in regattas in the Caribbean during the 1980s, and would realise they could be paid to do what they enjoyed. The advent of yacht chartering outside traditional Mediterranean cruising grounds created opportunities for a new generation of professional crew. Also, different destinations helped the business grow to accommodate clients whose preferences might include anything from the Pacific Islands to Patagonia. A growing industry, and larger yachts, called for a high calibre of captain, and increasingly skilled help from deck officers to engineers and chefs to stewardesses.

Not unnaturally, the demand for big yachts would ebb and flow with the circumstances of those able to afford them, and the political and economic climate of the day. A few yachts remain from the turn of the last century, and some others from the heady days of the 1930s. We have been fortunate to see an example of each in the shape of the schooner *Shenandoah* and the 'J' Class cutter *Velsheda*, both visitors to New Zealand during the 2000 America's Cup series. Their survival is a testament to the devotion of their respective owners, who obviously represent a much younger generation of yachtsmen.

Large yachts have always been among the privileges of the wealthy, and the industry has much to be thankful for lately, as new fortunes have been made in areas such as e-commerce and telecommunications. Indeed, the most significant reason for the proliferation of the super yachts, as we now know them, is the compact and reliable nature of modern satellite communications systems, which enable owners to remain in constant touch with their business interests. There is a trend towards bigger sailing yachts again, and this has been made possible by relatively recent advances in automated sail handling, which enable smaller crews to manage larger vessels. Motor yachts are growing too, due to advances in naval architecture, materials and propulsion systems, and the very largest are now helicopter-capable vessels in excess of 300 ft in length. There are more than 2500 yachts over 100 ft overall in commission around the world, and this number is presently increasing by 10 percent each year. Values range from below US$5 million to over US$100 million, and running expenses from 10–15 per cent of capital cost per annum. Crew numbers vary from five aboard a 100 ft yacht to more than 25 on a helicopter-carrying 300 footer.

This book presents some of the yachts that came to Auckland during the southern hemisphere summer of 1999/2000. There are vessels built in England, Germany, Holland, Italy, the United States, and New Zealand, which is now the world's fifth most prolific constructor of super yachts. Their history spans almost 100 years, from the launch of *Shenandoah* during 1902, to the christening of *Kokomo* in February 2000. I hope you will enjoy them all.

John Julian
April 2000

Shenandoah

'Sea Fever' and the schooner from Shooter's Island

I must go down to the seas again, to the vagrant gypsy life,

To the gull's way and the whale's way where the wind's like a whetted knife;

And all I ask is a merry yarn from a laughing fellow-rover,

And a quiet sleep and a sweet dream when the long trick's over.

FROM 'SEA FEVER' BY JOHN MASEFIELD (1902).

Masefield might well have had Shenandoah *in mind when he wrote his famous poem in 1902, as this was the year of the schooner's launch from the Townsend and Downey Shipyard in New York. Theodore Ferris designed her for the Wall Street financier Gibson Fahnestock, whose father, Harris, had helped the United States government obtain loans to pay for the Civil War. She was built alongside Kaiser Wilhelm's* Meteor III *at the yard on Shooter's Island, but would sail further, for longer, than any of the great yachts of her generation.*

Shenandoah first crossed the Atlantic during July of 1905, leaving New London and arriving at the Lizard, on the Cornish coast of England, 12 days later. Following a short stay in Brittany, she made for Kiel, where the German Navy was still in review after Kiel Week. From there she sailed for Copenhagen, and back to Hamburg, before concluding her summer cruise in Southampton, where she was laid up.

Fahnestock sold *Shenandoah* in 1912 to a German called Walter von Bruining who renamed the schooner *Lasca II*, and kept her in Kiel, which was also home to her sister *Meteor III*. Her new owner continued to sail, in spite of the advent of the First World War, and was cruising in British waters during the summer of 1915 when the yacht was appropriated by the British. She was detained until 1919 when Sir John Esplen acquired her, and reinstated her original name. Two years later, he would sell her to Godfrey H Williams of Southampton, who installed two Parsons paraffin engines, and used the yacht locally. But it was not until 1926 that she would really come into her stride, for it was then that the gloriously named Ludovico Spada Veralli Potenziani, Prince of Castelviscardo, bought her, changed her name to *Atlantide*, and took her to the Mediterranean. He sailed her from Italy to the Balearics, and on to Barcelona, participating in one of the first offshore regattas held in the Mediterranean. She then returned to Italy via the Greek Islands, where she was sold to the Danish philanthropist Viggo Jarl, who described the transaction as follows:

'The Prince invited me to Rome for a meeting. "Are you interested in my ship?" he asked. "I cannot deny it," I said. "Take it! Take it!" cried the Prince. And so I gave him a personal cheque on the spot. The yacht was mine with the silver, and all that was on board. That's the way things were handled between gentlemen in those days.'

Viggo Jarl would own *Atlantide* for some 25 years. He installed electricity and diesel engines soon after he bought her, and went on to sail around the Mediterranean, through the Red Sea, and down the coast of Sudan. He took her to the West Indies, and Colombia, and through the Panama Canal to Hawaii. And he voyaged to Buenos Aires and Rio de Janeiro, travelling 500 miles up the Amazon River during one extraordinary expedition in

Shenandoah's wheel and binnacle seen from the starboard quarter.

1937. Two years later, *Atlantide* was back in Europe cruising to the Faeroe and Shetland Islands, then via Germany into the Baltic to Poland where she remained in storage for some time with her masts out, and engines immobilised so that the Germans would not be able to commandeer her. Hermann Goering was known to be very keen on larger sailing yachts, and the Second World War was consuming Europe. But *Atlantide* was spared, and in 1946 she sailed for Africa to explore the Congo and Niger rivers during an excursion that was to last for eight months.

Many famous people visited the schooner during the course of Viggo Jarl's ownership. King Christian X was on board with Queen Alexandrine, and other guests included King Umberto of Italy, and King Baudouin of Belgium. The Duke of Windsor enjoyed *Atlantide* as well, exclaiming to Jarl on one occasion that 'I wish I could afford to buy this boat!' But having averaged some 18,000 n.m. per annum with his yacht, Viggo Jarl sold her in 1952, claiming that she required too much maintenance, and that good sailors were hard to find, and so *Atlantide* embarked on the most shadowy period of her long life.

From 1952 until 1969 *Atlantide*'s Owner of Record was the Compania de Navigacion San Augustin of Honduras. The schooner is known to have spent

Guests in period attire enjoy a sail to Kawau Island.

some of this time in Central and South America, where she was purportedly running contraband. She reappeared in the Mediterranean during 1962, and was impounded by the French government, apparently in lieu of some outstanding tax. She was to lie neglected for several more years before being rescued by Baron Marcel Bich and moved to the Voisin yard in Villefranche for an extensive refit under the supervision of Bich's celebrated Corsican skipper 'Captain Joe'. Her hull was stripped and lined with cork for insulation, she was re-rigged, Dacron sails were made, and new diesel engines installed. Bich renamed her *Shenandoah*, for he believed that, once christened, a yacht should keep her name forever.

The Baron also owned a fleet of 12 m yachts, and would mount a challenge for the America's Cup in 1974, so *Shenandoah* shaped a course for Newport, Rhode Island, almost 70 years after Gibson Fahnestock first sailed her there in 1905. She received a grand welcome home, and served as Bich's headquarters and as a spectator boat during the course of the campaign. She was to remain in the family's ownership until 1986, cruising the Mediterranean and the Caribbean, before being sold to Philippe Bommer, who eventually took her to Thailand where her present owner bought her in the summer of 1994.

The 'laughing fellow-rover' of Masefield's verse had now become *Shenandoah*'s captain, and it was he that brought the schooner to Auckland for the comprehensive restoration that lasted until the southern hemisphere autumn of 1996. Anyone who knows Serge Guilhaumou, *Shenandoah*'s Captain, will vouch for his good humour, and the tales he tells of his many years at sea are liberally punctuated with hoots of hilarity, regardless of whether he is describing a perfect trade wind passage, or a howling gale off Cape Horn.

Serge and his crew had nursed *Shenandoah* from South-east Asia to New Zealand, for she was once again in poor condition. But when she left for Fiji in September of 1996 she was alive with vigour and ready for a new adventure. She would enjoy a cracking sail from Viti Levu to Noumea, achieving 275 n.m. per day, pressing onward to Vanuatu and Papua

New Guinea via the Louisiade Archipelago. And she would traverse the Torres Strait between sunrise and sunset during one day in November before arriving in Darwin. From there she set off via Lombok and Bali to Phuket, and the King's Regatta, followed by some three months' cruising around Thailand, leaving for Sri Lanka, the Maldives, and the Chagos Archipelago at the beginning of April 1997.

Having skirted the Somalia coast, with its attendant pirates, *Shenandoah* made for Djibouti and the Sudanese port of Suakin. Here, another peal of laughter precedes Serge's description of several days spent in the ruins of this formerly important trading station. A misunderstanding with the local agent meant that three days were spent in a dilapidated courtroom, liberally sprinkled with goat droppings, until a tribunal could be assembled to decide whether *Shenandoah* could leave again. An interpreter was found, but he turned out to be Eritrean, and while apparently able to communicate directly with satellites in space, he could not make himself understood in court. Eventually tiring of this charade, the Chief Justice ruled that the yacht could go, and the agent was fined US$20.

Undaunted by this experience, the crew of *Shenandoah* set about exploring the extraordinary inland waterways further up the Sudanese coast. Having negotiated the reef at each entrance, it is possible to go as far as 3 n.m. into the desert. Serge recalls the incredible spectacle of an old man approaching the yacht in the 45 degree heat of the day, asking for food and water and, having offered his thanks, trudging away into the featureless waste of the hinterland.

Tracking northwards, *Shenandoah* would pass through the Suez Canal in a sandstorm before heading towards Turkey and the Greek Islands, southern Italy and Sardinia, and arriving in Cannes at the beginning of June. Following some remedial work in Marseilles, and a short cruise around Corsica, she embarked upon the annual round of Classic Yacht regattas at Imperia, Monaco, Cannes and St Tropez where she was much admired after many years' absence. She left in October 1997, stopping at Casablanca where she stayed for some days at the request of the royal family, before

Dolphin detail on the port guard rail aft.

moving on to the Canary Islands and the port of Dakar in Senegal. There followed a fast reach across to Salvador in Brazil, from where she headed down to the delightfully named Buzios, made famous during the 1960s by Brigitte Bardot, and on to Rio, and a berth in front of the Yacht Club.

Visits to Punta del Este, Montevideo, Buenos Aires, and Mar del Plata ensued before *Shenandoah* arrived at Peninsula Valdes, at the north-eastern extremity of Patagonia. Here the crew saw dolphins, orcas, penguins and sea lions before moving on to Comodoro Rivadavia for Christmas of 1998. This was to be the last of the T-shirt weather, however, and the climate became appreciably colder as the schooner moved into the Beagle Channel towards Ushuaia, and shortly thereafter Serge would go ashore to climb a glacier.

Shenandoah made for Cape Horn via Puerto Williams, and was greeted with fierce winds and big seas. But the schooner was soon on her way north again, with a spectacular cruise through the islands in prospect en route to Puerto Montt. *Shenandoah* would have whales for company, and beautiful anchorages such as the Laguna San Rafael, where she would tack through the growlers to the base of the glacier, and one of the most awe-inspiring backdrops for a sailing yacht anywhere in the world.

But the old schooner had scented warmer climes again, and she would

Shenandoah **is an unforgettable sight, and we may**

remember the thrust of her bow, the rake of her masts,

or the curve of her counter.

leave the coast of Chile for Robinson Crusoe and Easter Islands before stopping at Ducie, close to Pitcairn Island. By June 1999 she had reached the Marquesas Islands via Tahiti, to where she would return before leaving for Tonga and Fiji in July. Then she came back to Auckland, her South Pacific home, to be greeted by all that knew her, and those who had worked to make her young again. For there are many New Zealanders with a special affection for *Shenandoah* and her crew, and she has become an international symbol of the excellence of our maritime industries.

Aboard *Shenandoah*, you sail back into another time. Standing at her wheel, you can fully appreciate the clean sweep of her teak decks, which rise gently toward the base of her 9 m bowsprit. There is an abundance of historical detail, from the binnacle ahead of you, to the ornate bronze hinges on the skylights, and the pattern of the stanchions and belaying pins. You will marvel at the brilliance of her brightwork, and the faithful restoration of her deckhouses and topside furniture. And you will wonder at the intricacy of the standing and running rigging that adorns her varnished spars.

Below, in the saloon, you can almost hear the conversations that have taken place during the course of a century at sea. For *Shenandoah* has known war and peace, prosperity and poverty, joy and sadness. But she is happy now, and you can feel it in the fabric of the old schooner as you move through her accommodation. Her present owner 'wanted to respect the classical spirit of the yacht', and he has certainly succeeded, for while much of the vessel had to be recreated between 1994 and 1996, *Shenandoah* never lost her soul.

Her interior layout is mostly original, although some of the materials are subtly different. She is largely panelled in padouk wood, which contrasts beautifully with cream-coloured bulkheads, off-white carpets, and the warm, autumn shades of some of the soft furnishings.

The owner's stateroom is situated forward of the officers' quarters, which consist of two double cabins aft of the chart table towards the stern. Three guest staterooms are located off the central companionway between the master cabin and the saloon, where the dining table sits to starboard opposite a sofa and easy chairs, which lie to port. Forward of the saloon are the galley, crew mess, and accommodation for the remainder of the yacht's complement of 14.

The schooner's rigging conforms to the original pattern.

Leaving harbour, you are reminded of the need for a large crew for, with the exception of the two powered winches that are used to hoist the mizzen, *Shenandoah*'s sails are raised the traditional way, with block and tackle, and this exercise may take more than an hour to complete. Sitting in the deck saloon, under the removable roof, or standing in the shade of the awning that protects the helmsman from the sun, you will admire the practised ease of the ship's company. As she gathers way you will feel the same thrill that all who sailed her for so many years must have felt at the start of another voyage.

Shenandoah is an unforgettable sight, and we may remember the thrust of her bow, the rake of her masts, or the curve of her counter. But the lasting impression will be of timeless beauty, enduring character, and of majesty under sail.

In 2000 she will leave Auckland for the Mediterranean via Madagascar, and many are wondering where she will be for her centenary celebrations in 2002. All who have admired the yacht will have noticed her figurehead. He is a Native American from a tribe in the Shenandoah Valley. He looks far into the distance, and in his right hand holds a knife with which he goads the schooner forever onwards. So *Shenandoah* will probably be at sea, under full sail, loving life.

And where might Serge be? To quote John Masefield once again:

I must go down to the sea again, to the lonely sea and the sky,
And all I ask is a tall ship, and a star to steer her by.

Specifications

Value	Specification
54 m (177 ft 2 in.)	**LOA**
43 m (141 ft 1 in.)	**LOD**
41.18 m (135 ft 1 in.)	**LWL**
7.98 m (26 ft 2 in.)	**Beam**
4.7 m (15 ft 5 in.)	**Draught**
300 tonnes	**Displacement**
798 sq.m	**Sail area (upwind)**
2000 sq.m	**(downwind)**
Halsey Lidgard	**Sailmaker**
Harry Spencer	**Spars**
2 x 470 hp Lugger	**Engines**
2 x Northern Lights 55 kw	**Generators**
19,000 L	**Fuel**
Steel	**Construction**
Theodore E Ferris	**Designer**
Townsend & Downey, 1902	**Builder/Year**
McMullen & Wing, 1994–96	**Refit**

Shenandoah

Velsheda

A 'lady-in-waiting'

Velsheda *was built to contest the America's Cup, but her first appearance at the event would not happen until almost seven decades after her launch. The lady had endured a long wait, and there were times when her survival looked improbable, not to say impossible.*

The Solent is a temperamental body of water that lies between Hampshire, on the south coast of the English mainland, and the Isle of Wight. Ask anyone who grew up on its shores about the 'J' Class, and you may be told that the heyday of these majestic sloops was also the high-water mark of yacht racing. You may be lucky enough to find an octogenarian who served as a paid hand aboard Shamrock V, *or who helped to create her during 1930 at Camper and Nicholsons in Gosport, where* Velsheda *and* Endeavour *were also designed and built, in 1933 and 1934 respectively.*

Someone slightly younger might remember watching them from the front at Southsea, or the pier at Ryde, and seeing their sleek 40 m hulls cleaving the seas under the mighty wings of their Marconi rigs.

Anybody born after the Second World War would remember them too, but in a different light. *Shamrock V* had gone to the Mediterranean, and would not be seen in the Solent again until 1980, when she returned to Camper and Nicholsons. *Velsheda* had lain in a mud berth up the Hamble River since the late 1940s, her rig sold for scrap, and her position marked on the Admiralty Chart as a wreck. *Endeavour* had been abandoned on the Medina River, upstream from Cowes, and the Royal Yacht Squadron, under whose burgee she had challenged the American 'J' Class *Rainbow* for the America's Cup in 1934.

But it was not just the war, and the ensuing change in social history, that sounded the death knell for these great yachts. Although few people really noticed it at the time, it was when King George V's cutter *Britannia* was towed out into the English Channel and scuttled on 10 July 1936, after he had expired in January of that year. Designed by

GL Watson in 1893, *Britannia* had latterly been modified to rate under 'J' Class rules. Many felt that she had been the greatest British racing yacht ever built, and that something of the sport had died with her. There was to be no more 'J' Class racing in British waters after 1936, and, even in America, where six such yachts had been built, the days of this kind of competition were numbered.

Any child who saw these yachts in such distress during the 1950s and 1960s might have asked a parent what they were. One such child was Elizabeth Meyer, who would restore both *Shamrock V* and *Endeavour*, although it was not until she saw the latter at the old flying boat base at Calshot, across the Solent from Cowes, that the project gathered momentum. The old yacht had been moved there during the late 1970s in an earlier attempt at restoration, which had faltered due to lack of funds. And it was a man of this generation who boarded *Velsheda* at the Gosport yard of Camper and Nicholsons, over 60

Velsheda in company with the *Luna Rossa* yachts from the Prada 2000 America's Cup Challenge.

Velsheda

years after her launch from this very site, and bought her.

Velsheda had been built for Mr WL Stephenson of Woolworth fame and had been named after his three daughters, Velma, Sheila, and Daphne. While she never challenged for the America's Cup, she had given a good account of herself against the King's *Britannia*, as well as Sir Thomas Lipton's *Shamrock V*, and Sir TOM Sopwith's *Endeavour*. Along with many other large yachts, she was laid up for the duration of the Second World War, but was to stay in her Hamble mud berth, occasionally serving as a houseboat, until 1984, when she was rescued by an American who subsequently sold her to Terry Brabant. Brabant refitted her within his means, and equipped her with a new steel mast and a modest interior. Still without an engine, she plied for charter along the south coast of England, and occasionally ventured to the Mediterranean and the Caribbean. She was later sold to Philippe Bommer, a Swiss who had previously owned the three-masted schooner *Shenandoah*. She returned to Camper and Nicholsons for a further refit, but little was done due to an apparent shortage of money.

Her present owner and his young family bought *Velsheda* as a replacement for their existing 28 m yacht. It snowed the morning they viewed her, along with their captain, Simon Bolt, but the owner warmed to *Velsheda* as he paced her temporary plywood decks. His wife saw her husband's expression, and feared for his sanity, for she knew he had fallen in love. And so he had, shaking hands on the sale and the refit on that bitter January day in 1995.

There is no blueprint for the refit of a 'J' Class yacht, particularly when a racing owner also wants to cruise in comfort. For the 'J's were built for competition, and represented the leading edge of contemporary design, often incorporating technology and materials from the burgeoning aircraft industries of the 1930s. While they carried as many crew as the great racing schooners of the Edwardian era, they did not put to sea with pianos aboard, and had no fireplaces in the saloon. Accordingly, the modern designer has the relative luxury of 'carte blanche', tempered with the knowledge that the new interior should be in sympathy with the vintage character of the vessel.

It was to John Munford that the family turned, because of his company's reputation for finely detailed traditional interiors, as well as his success with *Endeavour*, and involvement with *Shamrock V*. Another challenge for those responsible for the rebirth of such a vessel is the relative lack of crew. While there may be more space to be used in a fo'c'sle that was once home to 30 men, the mechanical deck hardware and associated systems that have replaced these sailors take up space elsewhere in the hull, as do other equipment. *Velsheda*'s interior has been virtually sculptured in hand finished mahogany to fit around complicated structures and internal apparatuses. Raised and fielded panelling and walnut soles contrast beautifully with the cream paintwork of the deckhead and beams, reflecting the style and craftsmanship of the 1930s. Warm, traditional fabrics add to the welcoming atmosphere of the yacht, and the owner's collection of antiques and paintings contribute to the feeling of permanence that is part of her charm.

Gerard Dijkstra was appointed naval architect to the project, not least because of the similar role he had played in the reconstruction of both *Endeavour* and the schooner *Adela*. It was to be a challenging assignment, particularly as a great deal of modern equipment had to be incorporated in the rebuild. Dijkstra calculated that the yacht would lie lower in the water. His solution was to add 130 mm of extra hull plate above the original deck level, giving *Velsheda* the same freeboard as she had in 1933, albeit with a slightly longer waterline. Mindful of her racing pedigree, and her owner's competitive intentions, Dijkstra was able to achieve all this while keeping the yacht's dimensions, as well as her underbody, within the letter of the 'J' Class rules.

While the owner was determined to retain the original spirit of the vessel, he naturally wanted his family to be safe. Accordingly, *Velsheda* incorporates three watertight bulkheads as well as a 17-zone fire fighting system. Captain Bolt had other plans as well. 'With five years' experience on the last boat, we knew how *Velsheda* would be used. From the start, I was adamant about an aft cockpit. When the owner is at the wheel, his kids are right next to him. You can't have children on the open aft deck of a 'J' Class yacht whose quarter wave approaches the cap rail.' Bolt therefore specified such a cockpit, as well as a small doghouse, forward of the wheel, containing a chart table. This was built, along with the main deckhouse, skylights and hatches, in period style. The deckhouse offers a snug refuge with a good view in less than clement weather, and is entered from a roomy cockpit aft, which is ideal for outside dining.

Elsewhere on deck, you will notice over 20 winches, the largest of which stand like sentinels in line, astern, either side of the mast. All can be switched from hydraulic to manual when necessary. These 'silent deckhands', to use Gerard Dijkstra's expression, enable four crew out of a total of six to do what 30 men did when *Velsheda* was new. Twenty of them were needed on the halyard to hoist the mainsail, but although the present Vectran sail weighs but one third of the 3000 lb original, loading it onto the 'Park Avenue' boom still takes the best part of a day. Foresails are attached by means of alloy pins that clip into carbon fibre hanks permanently attached to the headstay. But the most impressive single item is the spar. Beautifully faired, and towering some 50 m above the deck, the mast is made of carbon fibres of such high strength and modulus that its weight is less than half of an alloy equivalent. Other exotic materials to be found aboard *Velsheda* include titanium in sail headboards and flying blocks, and carbon graphite stabilised bearing material in items of rigging and deck hardware.

Back at Southampton Yacht Services there was a deadline to be met. *Velsheda* would race *Endeavour* once again, over 60 years after their last meeting. This time it was to be in Antigua, rather than the Solent, at the annual Classics Regatta in April of 1998. During the final months of the refit, yard personnel would work three shifts to finish the yacht on schedule. And *Velsheda* would win, beating her sister and all the other yachts competing on handicap in her class.

As remarkable as this achievement was, *Velsheda* was only just getting back into her stride. By the end of the following year she would be in Auckland to witness the thirtieth America's Cup Defence, some 66 years after the series she had been built to contest. She

Specifications

LOA	39.5 m (129 ft 6 in.)
LWL	27.1 m (88 ft 11 in.)
Beam	6.57 m (21 ft 6 in.)
Draught	4.8 m (15 ft 9 in.)
Sail area (main)	462 sq.m
(genoa)	358 sq.m
Mast	Carbospars
Mast height	50.25 m (164 ft 10 in.)
Winches	Lewmar
Engine	MTU 420 hp
Generators	2 x 45 kw Northern Lights
Fuel	5000 L
Construction	Steel hull, aluminium deck
Classification	Maltese Cross 100A1 Yacht* LMC
Naval architects	CE Nicholson / G Dijkstra
Interior design	John Munford
Builder/Year	Camper and Nicholsons, 1933
	Southampton Yacht Services, 1997

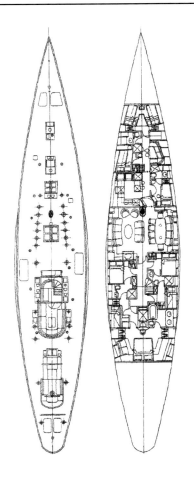

had cruised the Pacific in company with her escort, a handsome 33 m Feadship built in 1962 for Henry Ford II, and originally named *Santa Maria*. Like *Velsheda*'s original tender, she is now called *Bystander*, and together they would visit Panama, the Galapagos and Tahiti on their way to New Zealand. In Auckland, *Velsheda* would show her pace again, comfortably leading the opposition during the Logan Classic, and for much of the New Zealand Millennium Cup Regatta which attracted the largest gathering of super yachts ever seen in the southern hemisphere.

She left Auckland in early March 2000, in company with *Bystander*, for Australia, the Maldives, Suez, and the Mediterranean to complete a circumnavigation that Charles E Nicholson could never have envisaged for her in 1933. He could hardly have imagined that her first appearance at the America's Cup would not happen until almost seven decades had elapsed since her launch, or that it would take place in New Zealand. But he would have been pleased at the way she stole the show.

The lady had indeed endured a long wait. But she returned, and now delights a younger generation with her grace and her power. We are fortunate to see her like again.

Velsheda

Aschanti IV of Vegesack

Wanted: a north wind

Davies sniffed the wind and scanned the tree tops, where light gusts were toying with the leaves.

'Sou'-west still,' he said, 'and more rain coming. But it's bound to shift into the north.'

'Will that be a good wind for us?'

'It depends where we go,' he said slowly.

FROM 'THE RIDDLE OF THE SANDS' BY ROBERT ERSKINE CHILDERS (1903)

Davies and his friend Carruthers were aboard the *Dulcibella*, their adventure described by Robert Erskine Childers in his 1903 novel, *The Riddle of the Sands*. The north wind was to take them back to the East Frisian Islands, which run west from Cuxhaven, where the River Weser joins the North Sea. Further up the Weser lies Vegesack, just short of Bremen, Germany's oldest maritime city. In Vegesack, Jacht & Bootswerft Burmester built the schooner yacht *Aschanti IV* during 1954. She would sail for 40 years, before returning to the yard, now known as Fr. Lurssen Werft, for a comprehensive refit. And then the north wind would take her across the Atlantic, and through the Panama Canal to the Pacific Ocean beyond.

Ernst Burmester created *Aschanti IV* to race, and she proved to be one of the fastest and most beautiful yachts of her era. She was built of flush-riveted steel, with a 30-ton cast iron and lead keel, to a Henry Gruber design. Burmester campaigned her vigorously until shortly before he died, and his widow sold her to the first of a number of owners who cruised her. She returned to Germany in 1987, where a new deck was fitted, before she was placed on the charter market as *Aschanti of Saba*.

She was subsequently neglected, however, and by 1992 was lying in New Bedford, Massachusetts, on the north-eastern seaboard of the United States. She was no longer seaworthy, much of her hull plating needed to be replaced, and her future looked bleak. But a yachtsman who had admired her under sail on the River Weser, many years before, had learned of her plight. He bought her, and shipped her home to Vegesack on the deck of a freighter.

The story of her restoration is remarkable, and involved men who had been brought out of retirement to practise their riveting skills once more. She was to receive hollow spruce spars with stainless steel fittings made from original templates. Her engine was replaced, three new generators installed, and modern electronic equipment fitted. The original interior layout specified by Ernst Burmester was little changed, but extensively refitted with rich, polished mahogany. Deck hardware was largely replaced with Lewmar electric winches, although some original items remain. All of this was achieved in the space of 12 months, and *Aschanti IV of Vegesack* would sail from the Lurssen Shipyard in the early summer of 1994. She would cruise throughout that summer, arriving in St Tropez for the celebrated Nioulargue Regatta in October, where she won the Florida Cup Trophy. *Aschanti* then wintered in the Caribbean, taking part in the Antigua Classic Yacht Regatta the following April, before returning to the Mediterranean, where she would stay until the autumn of 1997.

Some years after her owner had noticed *Aschanti IV* on the Weser, a Dutch boy joined the Sea Scouts in Grootebroek, on the Ijsselmeer, at the western end of the Frisian Islands. Derek Desaunois was to become a professional skipper, and would join *Aschanti* as captain in October of 1997, with some 10 trans-Atlantic crossings and a trip to the Pacific already behind him.

Following a winter season in the Caribbean, Derek took the schooner through the Panama Canal and up to Vancouver, from where she cruised as far north as the Alaskan border. Arriving in Victoria, on Vancouver Island, *Aschanti* found herself in the middle of a vintage yacht regatta, and

OPPOSITE

The schooner was refitted
with hollow spruce spars
and rigging made from
original templates during
her 1993 restoration.

BELOW

Wheel and binnacle.

was asked to participate. She raced, and, in light airs, finished second to another schooner, called *Barlovento*, also drawn by Henry Gruber. As Gruber was far from prolific as a designer, this was a happy coincidence indeed!

Aschanti spent Christmas and the New Year in San Diego at the end of her summer cruise, before shaping a course for Auckland via the Cook Islands. Her subsequent presence in Westhaven was a welcome bonus for admirers of immaculately maintained classic yachts, and a credit to the commitment of her owner and his crew.

You may well have admired the schooner during her stay. Her striking black hull, with its white boot topping, contrasts beautifully with the abundant brightwork of her deckhouse, skylights and spars. A wooden tender sits on deck, below the main staysail boom, and items of deck hardware such as cleats, made to a traditional pattern, and belaying pins enhance the vintage quality of her appearance. Moving through the bright and spacious deck saloon, where the owner's party of six can dine in comfort while enjoying a panoramic view, you descend to the companionway dividing the main accommodation. The owner's suite, comprising office, stateroom and bath, has always been to starboard, but the guest accommodation to port, along with the cabin occupied by Derek and his New Zealand wife, Leanne, are more recent additions. Among the fixtures on this side of the hull during *Aschanti*'s early racing days was a large sewing machine with which the crew made running repairs to sails torn in the chase. Further forward lies the crew mess and galley, along with the fo'c'sle, which is home to the schooner's four additional crew.

We hoped *Aschanti IV of Vegesack* would linger here but, while she may no longer need a north wind to take her onwards, her itinerary is not yet fixed. As Davies would say, slowly: 'It depends where we go.'

Specifications

LOA	31.4 m (103 ft)
LWL	22 m (72 ft 2 in.)
Beam	6.38 m (23 ft)
Draught	4.3 m (14 ft 1 in.)
Displacement	135 tons
Sail area	509 sq.m
Masts	Spruce
Foremast height	31 m (101 ft 7 in.)
Main mast height	34 m (111 ft 6 in.)
Winches	Lewmar
Engine	MTU 504 hp diesel
Construction	Flush-riveted steel
Naval architect	Henry Gruber
Builder/Year	Jacht & Bootswerft Burmester, 1954

Itasca

A 'true beginning' … and glorious fulfilment

There must be a beginning of any great matter, but the continuing unto the end until it be thoroughly finished yields the true glory.

SIR FRANCIS DRAKE (1587)

Sir Francis Drake wrote these words during his country's long war with Spain. They were worthy of being repeated during the afternoon of 26 August 1994, for Itasca had just traversed the North-West Passage from west to east, becoming the first private yacht to achieve this distinction in a single season. The voyage had started 23 days earlier in Port Clarence, Alaska, and would conclude that night as the vessel steamed up the Sondre Stromfjord on the West Coast of Greenland. It had been a challenging, sometimes harrowing, but infinitely rewarding expedition for the ship's company, and the realisation of an ambition long held by Bill Simon, Itasca's owner, and United States Treasury Secretary from 1974 to 1977.

The name *Itasca* is derived from the Latin for 'true beginning', which seems entirely appropriate for the new life she started in 1980. She had been built in 1961 by J & K Smits Scheepswerven of Kinderdijk, Holland, as an ocean-going salvage tug, one of the most powerful of her kind at the time. She was named *Thames*, and would serve the famous Dutch company in the worst of the world's weather, fighting her way through violent storms to reach ships in distress, and hauling the casualties across thousands of miles of open sea. She would tow on contract as well, transporting oil rigs, dry docks or vessels destined for the breakers, and it was at the end of one such trip to the South Atlantic that her conversion came to pass.

Her new owner was looking for what is now known as a 'discovery yacht', one that is self-sufficient, immensely seaworthy, and able to explore the extremities of latitude and climate. He might not have known that *Thames'* transformation would establish a trend, for while commercial vessels and even warships had been adapted for private use, nobody had done this with a large tug. The vessel returned to Holland to have her towing gear removed, and the bulk of the structural work undertaken. The newly christened *Itasca* then set off for Seattle, where the conversion was completed in time for a trip to the West Indies during the northern hemisphere winter of 1982. But *Itasca* was not to reach her full potential, and for the 10 years that followed she visited the Mediterranean only once. Otherwise, she would cruise the west coast of the United States, spending her summers in Alaska, and wintering in Mexico.

During this time, Bill Simon and his captain, Allan Jouning, had been enjoying the Sparkman and Stephens designed ketch *Freedom*, which they had built at Cantieri Picchiotti in Viareggio during 1985. But as he sailed around the world, Simon had been thinking of the North-West Passage, and wondering whether his 38 m yacht could be strengthened to cope with the ice. One day, at his home in Hawaii, Simon was reading a nautical magazine and noticed a converted tug for sale in Mexico. He called Allan Jouning, who was at home in New Zealand overseeing *Freedom*'s refit, and Allan flew to Puerto Vallarta to look over *Itasca*. A price was agreed, and Bill Simon took delivery of his new yacht in May of 1993.

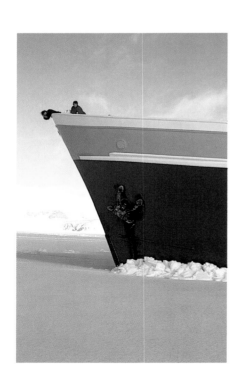

Itasca **in the Antarctic, 1995.**

The project was now in progress, and Allan took the boat to Alaska for a period of evaluation. By June, *Itasca* was in Seattle, where she was substantially refitted in anticipation of the voyage to come. During the next 12 months, a series of structural and plating modifications were made to strengthen this already rugged vessel for her arctic adventure. Equipment was also readied: radar scanners and air horns would have to be heated, as would the watermakers and most of the plumbing. *Itasca*'s central ballast tank would be used as a reservoir for engine and generator cooling so that ice sludge would not be ingested from the sea. Her stabiliser fins would be a liability in the ice, so a way to remove them under water had to be found. Crew quarters and bridge would be stripped and rebuilt, the latter to accommodate the most advanced communications and navigational equipment available. Judy Bell Davis would supervise the redecoration of the guest quarters with Bill Simon's wife and daughter-in-law. And the upper deck aft would be modified to take a helicopter. It was a Herculean undertaking, but, by June of 1994, *Itasca* was ready.

Bill Simon had also been busy assembling a group of friends who would join Allan Jouning's crew of 12. *Itasca* then moved north again during June

and July on a cruise that took her across the Barents Sea to Russia. Her guests left to make final preparations before rejoining the vessel on 3 August in Port Clarence, Alaska, after plans to board at Nome had been changed due to adverse weather conditions. Later that day, *Itasca* steamed into the Bering Strait to begin a journey that would earn her a place in the history of the North-West Passage, almost 88 years after the Norwegian Roald Amundsen first found a way through. She flew the flags of the Explorers Club and the United Nations during the historic voyage.

But *Itasca* and her crew would have little time to reflect upon their unique achievement for, incredibly, she would be in antarctic waters five months later, having paused for only a few weeks in New York. She passed through the Straits of Magellan, round Cape Horn and set off across Drake Passage to the southernmost continent before returning to Puerto Montt through the Chilean archipelago. Next she embarked for Auckland on a journey that took four weeks at 10 knots along latitude 42 degrees south, which links New Zealand's North Island with Puerto Montt. Indeed latitude would figure largely in Allan Jouning's logs during his first year in command of Bill Simon's *Itasca*, for the vessel had reached 75 degrees north in the Arctic, and 68 degrees south in the Antarctic.

Itasca spent the southern hemisphere winter of 1995 in refit before leaving Auckland for a Pacific Island cruise. By February of the following year she was back in familiar

Itasca is no stranger to extremes of latitude.

Alaskan waters. Moving down the west coast of the United States and Mexico, she entered the Caribbean via the Panama Canal where she spent an agreeable season before steaming north for Long Island for some summer fun with her owner. But a new chapter in her life was soon to open, for Allan Jouning had devised a charter itinerary that would take her around the world. By November 1997 she was in Patagonian waters, and would soon renew her acquaintance with the Antarctic, delighting her many charter guests who had long wanted the chance to go further afield. This, they agreed, was what a 'discovery yacht' was meant to do. She then made the long journey up to the Baltic for more charters during the northern hemisphere summer of 1998 before leaving for the Mediterranean to spend September and October. Passing through the Suez Canal in November, she would be back in New Zealand in time for Christmas. Following a short period of remedial work in Auckland, she would shape a course for Tahiti and the French Society Islands, before returning to New Zealand via Fiji for the America's Cup.

You know that you are going to experience something special before you see *Itasca*, for her exploits during the seven years of Bill Simon's ownership have conferred an almost legendary status upon the vessel, her captain and crew. She has covered 130,000 n.m. since May 1993 in the course of two world circuits, and has accomplished several yachting firsts, including the only circumnavigation of both the North and South American continents.

You will recognise her at once, for she has an aura of power and purpose that sets her apart from other super yachts. Her heritage is unmistakable, but unlike the other tugs that have subsequently been converted, her topsides are glossy and her superstructure stylish. The brilliant white of her upper works serves to mask the loft of the sundeck lounge below the helipad which, together with the lower saloon underneath, was built upon what was once *Itasca*'s towing deck. Indeed the lines of her hull were faithfully followed during the course of her conversion, from the deck extensions behind the existing accommodation to the sloping curve of the windows in the after main deck lounge. If you look at a plan of the vessel as she was built, you will see that the external appearance of the bridge is little changed, except for the absence of the gun-like fire monitor. She was built to take whatever the elements could throw at her, and it shows.

Boarding *Itasca* on the starboard main deck, you can make your way directly to the aft deck lounge. This is situated on what was the after section of the towing deck, and you are reminded of this by the presence of an original warping capstan which has been converted into a raised table. The view is spectacular, for large, toughened glass windows follow the line of the gunwales to each side, and around the semi-circle of the transom. Comfortable sofas face inward and aft, and guests can enjoy lunch at tables arranged forward and to either side of the capstan.

ABOVE

One of the five staterooms in the guest quarters.

BELOW

The dining room.

Itasca

Standing behind the wooden wheel, you try to imagine a little of what the captain has witnessed over the last seven years . . . you see polar bears and whales in the icy extremes . . .

Entering the main saloon through the double doors in the after bulkhead, you are reminded of a drawing room in a country lodge. Mahogany bookshelves line the starboard bulkhead below the windows, while big sofas and easy chairs to port invite you to relax with a book from the yacht's extensive library. The atmosphere is welcoming and informal, comfortable but unembellished. The forward dining area is similarly unadorned, being simply furnished with a fine mahogany table and period chairs. This is your first clue to the understated nature of the vessel. For *Itasca* has nothing to prove, as the framed map of her world travels on the dining room bulkhead will attest. Take a little time to absorb the scope of her voyages, and those of her predecessor *Freedom*, and you will begin to appreciate the remarkable collection of artwork and photography to be found throughout the ship.

Moving forward on the starboard side, and skirting the galley to port, the companionway leads to the four guest staterooms, each with adjoining dressing room and bathroom with tub. All have chairs, desks and tables which give you the impression of being in a small apartment, rather than a large cabin.

Making your way aft the central stairway leads down to the crew mess, accommodation, and engine room. There are six double crew cabins, each with adjacent heads and showers, along with a galley and dining area. Further aft in the engine room are the two original, nine cylinder Smit-MAN diesels and three 190 kW Caterpillar generators. The main engines produce 1250 shaft horsepower apiece and can drive the massive single screw individually or in tandem. They are as beautifully maintained as the rest of the equipment aboard *Itasca* and feature open rocker gear, which requires manual oiling at regular intervals. Engineer Hector Arceo has been tending the yacht's machinery since before Bill Simon bought her, and she has not missed a beat during this time.

The sundeck is two levels above the engine room, and the stairway takes you up to the after saloon. This commodious area is furnished in the same style as the main saloon below, with further evidence of Bill Simon's extensive travels on display. Not surprisingly, the sundeck is popular with guests in warm weather, and you can dine in the shade of the helicopter platform through the glass doors in the after bulkhead, or sit in the open on the settees and reclining chairs further aft. The superstructure narrows forward of the stairwell, and *Itasca*'s two 8.5 m tenders sit to each side of this passage while the vessel is under way. The forward section of the sundeck, below the bridge, contains the owner's suite, which includes a bedroom, dressing room and bathroom, along with a large dayroom complete with fireplace.

Captain Allan Jouning's quarters are overhead, behind the bridge and chart/radio room, and consist of a stateroom, day room, and bathroom. The bridge itself is panelled throughout in teak, and is a blend of Dutch tradition with the very latest instruments and systems. Standing behind the wooden wheel, you try to imagine a little of what the captain has witnessed over the last seven years. You see polar bears and whales in the icy extremes of latitude, the palm-fringed beaches and crystal-clear waters that lie closer to the equator, and the heavy weather in between. And you conjure up images of mountainous seas and hurricane-force winds that faced the Smit tug masters as they strove to get lines aboard casualties during the 19 years that this vessel was called *Thames*.

Leaving the wheelhouse, you climb the stairs to the flying bridge. Another ship's wheel stands behind a weathered compass on a pedestal, with Satellite A and M domes mounted fore and aft. A further expanse of teak deck, forward of the funnel, marks the after extremity of the open bridge. There is a small platform you can stand on, just in front of the mast. You could see the world from here; indeed some of Bill Simon's many friends already have.

Specifications

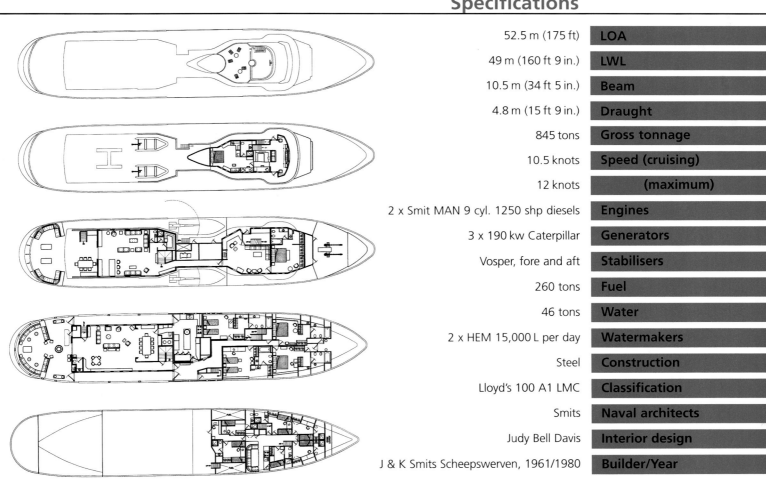

52.5 m (175 ft)	**LOA**
49 m (160 ft 9 in.)	**LWL**
10.5 m (34 ft 5 in.)	**Beam**
4.8 m (15 ft 9 in.)	**Draught**
845 tons	**Gross tonnage**
10.5 knots	**Speed (cruising)**
12 knots	**(maximum)**
2 x Smit MAN 9 cyl. 1250 shp diesels	**Engines**
3 x 190 kw Caterpillar	**Generators**
Vosper, fore and aft	**Stabilisers**
260 tons	**Fuel**
46 tons	**Water**
2 x HEM 15,000 L per day	**Watermakers**
Steel	**Construction**
Lloyd's 100 A1 LMC	**Classification**
Smits	**Naval architects**
Judy Bell Davis	**Interior design**
J & K Smits Scheepswerven, 1961/1980	**Builder/Year**

Seljm

La dolce vita

Ask any connoisseur of the finer things in life which country embodies the pursuit of beauty and style, and the answer would probably be Italy. Most seafarers would be happy to admit that a schooner represents the epitome of grace under sail, and that, ideally, such a vessel should be made out of wood. Those fortunate enough to contemplate the purchase of such a yacht would only be satisfied with the product of a shipyard with a tradition of excellence. Cantieri Sangermani of Lavagna, on the Ligurian coast of north-west Italy is such a yard, and it was here in 1978 that Seljm was conceived to the design of the famous naval architect Franco Anselmi Boretti.

She was launched in June 1980 as Yard No. 203, her teak hull measuring 29 m, with an overall length of 34 m including her bowsprit, making her the longest yacht built by Cantieri Sangermani in over 80 years of activity.

Nobody is quite sure when 'Dorin' Sangermano built his first boat, but he won a gold medal at an exhibition held at Bagni di Montecatini in the summer of 1906 for a small sailing craft that he had entered. His two sons, Cesare and Piero, whose surname became Sangermani as a result of a mistake made by a registration official, continued the family boat building tradition, and competed successfully in many regattas around the Gulf of Genoa, and along the Côte d'Azur. The exact number of vessels built by 'Dorin' Sangermano before 1945 is also unknown, as records were lost during the Second World War, but Cesare Sangermani Jr, presently head of the company, estimates that some 100 left the yard at Mulinetti. Cesare and Piero built a further 40, having moved the yard to Rapallo in 1934, and nearly 250 have emerged from the Lavagna premises, established during 1946, when Yard No. 1, *Nibbio II*, was launched. Many of the Lavagna yachts have achieved recognition through racing successes, such as the classic 28 m yawl *Gitana IV*, while others have been admired as the most elegant cruising craft of their generation.

Seljm was built for an Italian yachtsman from Genoa, and was cruised extensively throughout the Mediterranean with the owner, his family and friends. She made one return trip to the Caribbean during this period of her life, which spanned 15 years. During the early 1990s, *Seljm* caught the eye of Patrick Monteiro de Barros, a former Olympic sailor and current International Dragon champion who is also Commodore of the Club Naval de Cascais near Lisbon in Portugal. In October 1995 he bought her, and, following a period of remedial work at the Sangermani yard, she set off for the Caribbean under the command of Steve Ray, a native of Ohio in the United States, with many years' experience as a captain of ocean-going sailing yachts.

At the conclusion of her winter season in the West Indies, *Seljm* sailed for the north-eastern seaboard by way of Savannah, Georgia, where she underwent a short refit. Among

the high points of the pleasant summer that followed was her victory in the annual Chesapeake Schooner Race, which yielded a handsome trophy to add to her owner's extensive collection. She returned to the Caribbean once again for the winter of 1996/97, cruising the Dominican Republic and Cuba, before sailing from Jamaica to Cartagena in Colombia, again with the owner aboard. Following her transit of the Panama Canal, *Seljm* headed north for Costa Rica and Islas de Chiriqui. She then set off for the Cocos, the Marquesas, and French Polynesia, where she was based for three months at the Marina Taina in Tahiti, while exploring the Society Islands and the Tuamoto Archipelago.

Seljm reached New Zealand by way of Tonga in the early southern hemisphere summer of 1997/98 and was based at the Maritime Museum in Auckland for some months before returning to Tonga and Fiji. Happily for those who enjoy the sight of such

a lovely yacht on the Waitemata, she returned to her base on the eastern side of Hobson Wharf, where she would remain for some time. Her presence was also a source of great pleasure for the staff of the Maritime Museum, which has received several valuable exhibits and other considerations from her generous owner.

Anyone admiring *Seljm* can satisfy themselves that she was built at Cantieri Sangermani without having to ask, for at each end of the gold cove stripe on her brilliant white hull, there are three dots, representing the Morse letter 'S'. This trademark extends to the Club Sangermani burgee, worn by many yachts built at the Lavagna yard, which features the gold dots against a sky blue background with a darker blue border. Once aboard, you will detect other clues among the beautifully crafted fittings and rich panelling of the interior, along with special items of deck hardware. Standing at her raised helmsman's station, surrounded by a high, varnished coaming, you look forward along a broad expanse of pristine teak towards the elegant coach roof above her main saloon, which is also agleam with brightwork. On the open deck between the superstructures there is comfortable seating and a table for 'al fresco' dining. Within the steering cockpit there are settees to each side under the bimini top below the main boom, and aft of these is a further small, coach roof on the quarter deck with a hatch leading down to the chart table and ship's office. The monkey rail and the transom are varnished, as are the shallow bulwarks, which extend to the base of *Seljm*'s bowsprit, as well as her masts and booms.

Moving forward and down the companionway on the starboard side of the after coach roof bulkhead, you reach the main saloon, which features large windows on either side for a good view of the surroundings. The exposed deckhead beams are typical of Sangermani yachts, and their darker hue contrasts well with the honey colours of the furniture and the bright fabrics of the upholstery. The saloon table is forward and to port, with an 'L' shaped settee, chairs, and a small bench affording comfortable dining for eight guests.

Aft of the saloon, and down another companionway, are four cabins, which are reached from a central passage. They are more or less the same size, which is ideal for a charter party of four couples, and each has an adjoining head and shower. One has a bathtub as well, for those who want to have a whisky and a more leisurely wash after an arduous day's sailing, or playing with the various 'water toys' that are part of *Seljm*'s comprehensive inventory.

Going forward once again, you reach the galley and crew quarters via the companionway

beyond the dining area in the saloon, although the crew has separate access through a hatch on the foredeck. The captain's accommodation is to starboard, past the galley, and the crew berths are situated in the fo'c'sle, along with heads and shower. *Seljm* sails with a complement of five, and their make-up is typically multinational. Captain Steve Ray and Jessica Devreux, who comes from the Bahamas, employ a first mate, a chief engineer, and a stewardess, any of whom may be of American, Antipodean, or European extraction.

Seljm would appear to embody Cesare Sangermani's credo of 'Technology and Tradition', for, in addition to her comfort, classic appearance and impressive sailing performance, she offers heating and air conditioning as well as state-of-the-art telecommunications and entertainment facilities. The active charterer may also make use of a tender for water skiing, or a windsurfer between snorkelling and scuba diving sessions, while the lazy can recline in the shade of the awning with a good book and a large drink.

Seljm has enjoyed a lengthy sojourn in New Zealand, and will set sail for Vanuatu, New Caledonia, and the Great Barrier Reef before making for Sydney and the Olympic Games. Her voyage will continue via Cairns and Darwin to Phuket, the Maldives, Goa, and the Red Sea. Then she will return to the Mediterranean for the first time in almost six years. But there will be little rest for this stylish schooner, for her owner is planning to contest the trans-Atlantic race that is scheduled to start from Sandy Hook on 18 May 2002.

There were many fine yachts in Auckland for the America's Cup series, but few were as beautiful as *Seljm*. For those who saw her during her stay, she will always be a happy memory, but for those who sail her, life will seem very sweet indeed.

Specifications

34 m (111 ft 7 in.)	**LOA**
29 m (95 ft 2 in.)	**LOD**
7.01 m (23 ft)	**Beam**
3.6 m (11 ft 9 in.)	**Draught**
117 tonnes	**Displacement**
Caterpillar 365 hp diesel	**Engine**
48 kw Caterpillar, 16 kw Onan	**Generators**
6000 L	**Fuel**
Teak	**Construction**
Franco Anselmi Boretti	**Designer**
Cantieri Sangermani, 1980	**Builder/Year**

Seljm

Andromeda la Dea

Legend of a sea goddess

According to Greek mythology, Andromeda was the daughter of King Cepheus and Queen Cassiope. Pride in her daughter's good looks led Cassiope to assert that Andromeda was more beautiful than the Nereids. Enraged at this slight, Poseidon sent a sea monster to devastate Cepheus's kingdom and, since only Andromeda's sacrifice would appease the angry gods, she was chained to a rock, and left to be devoured by the monster. Fortunately for her, Perseus was flying by on his winged horse, Pegasus. Falling for the damsel in distress, he asked her father, Cepheus, for her hand. Cepheus agreed, and Perseus slew the monster.

ABOVE

All the sailing and engine
controls seen here are
duplicated on the flying bridge.

Like Perseus, Tom Perkins is an admirer of beauty, and, while he may not have a flying horse, he has owned some of the most important supercharged sports cars of the 1930s including rare examples of leading marques such as Alfa Romeo, Bugatti, Duesenberg, and Mercedes-Benz. Two of his yachts were built during the early part of the last century as well: the 1915, Nat Herreshoff designed, 39 m schooner *Mariette*, and her tender, the 1930, Alfred Mylne designed, 37.3 m motor yacht *Atlantide*. Following a major refit during 1995 at Cantieri Beconcini in La Spezia, *Mariette* has been a regular competitor at the foremost vintage regattas, and contested the 1997 Trans-Atlantic Challenge. She was normally escorted by Tom Perkins' modern yacht, the 1990, Perini Navi built, 47 m ketch *Andromeda la Dea*, until he realised that these fixtures were interfering with his world cruising itinerary, which is what *Andromeda*, his second Perini vessel of that name, had been built for. Accordingly, he decided 'that, clearly, I needed another boat', and, having found *Atlantide* lying neglected in Malta, he set about restoring her to act as *Mariette*'s companion.

Andromeda la Dea had already sailed around the world by 1994, the first of the Perini Navi yachts to do so. She left Viareggio on the first day of the northern hemisphere spring of 1991 on a journey that would take more than three years. Having visited

England and Norway, she embarked for Newport, Rhode Island, on the north-eastern seaboard of the United States, encountering heavy weather off the Atlantic provinces of Canada during the tempest that was immortalised by the author Sebastian Junger in his 1997 book *The Perfect Storm*. Don Lessels, *Andromeda*'s captain, was later to report that the water had been knee deep on the flying bridge. Moving south into balmier climes, she entered the Pacific via the Panama Canal before making for San Francisco, where she would spend six months. From there she cruised to the western coast of Canada and shaped a course for Hawaii and Fiji, arriving in Auckland at the end of 1993. She left New Zealand from Wellington early the following year, visiting Sydney, Brisbane, Cairns, and Darwin, before embarking for the Seychelles, a three-week trip made on one tack, broken only by a 24-hour stop in the Cocos Islands for running repairs to some sails. *Andromeda la Dea* would return to Viareggio during the Mediterranean summer of 1994, where Tom Perkins was presented with a gold medal, struck by Fabio Perini to commemorate this inaugural circumnavigation.

Simon Potter had served as engineer aboard the yacht for much of this time, and would become her captain following Don Lessels' retirement, and the conclusion of *Andromeda*'s subsequent refit later that year. A native of Devonport, Simon was raised in

Birkenhead on Auckland's North Shore, and, like many New Zealanders, had spent much of his youth racing boats. Nevertheless, as he candidly admits, he was pleasantly surprised, at the age of 29, when Tom Perkins 'handed me the keys and said "See you in Antigua"'. During his five years in command, Simon has enhanced the yacht's reputation for serious voyaging, taking her from established cruising grounds to more remote destinations, including Alaska and Antarctica during the course of one year. And he has maintained the vessel's self-reliant character, with his crew undertaking much of the work that would normally be left to the yard, which makes *Andromeda la Dea*'s spotless appearance even more remarkable. In automotive terms, taking this yacht to the extremes of latitude could be likened to entering the London to Sydney Rally in a Bentley. It can be done (as Keith Schellenberg demonstrated during 1968) but it takes a special kind of competitor, and plenty of commitment.

She might explore the coast of Thailand, or the pristine

cruising grounds of Myanmar. But sail she will, for that is what

this beauty was born to do.

Most would agree that *Andromeda la Dea* is one of the most attractive vessels of her size in the world. Her silver superstructure sits lightly upon a dark blue hull whose conventional lines belie her power. Tom Perkins takes a special interest in the development of his yachts, and his influence can be found aloft as well as below. Boarding over the graceful stern with its conventional transom, you descend into the cockpit by way of four shallow steps bracketed by settees. Forward, and amidships is a dining table, and the saloon is accessible from either side of the central, aft-facing bar. Here, a fine marine oil painting is situated above the fireplace, between bookshelves, in the forward bulkhead. Two tables stand in the middle of the saloon, with red leather sofas and easy chairs to each side. Forward, and to starboard, you pass a short stairway leading to the wheelhouse before entering the dining room and bar, which offers a panoramic view over the foredeck and to either side. Here, as in the saloon, red leather upholstery and a neutral carpet enhance the natural warmth of the exquisitely crafted teak panelling.

Below, guest accommodation consisting of two double cabins and one twin is accessed from a central lobby. A fourth door, aft and to port, leads to the owner's study and on to his stateroom with its two adjacent bathrooms. The spacious feel of these quarters is amplified by judicious use of mirrors and soft lighting, together with white headlining which also serves to accent the rich teak furniture and the understated fabrics.

The most direct route to the flying bridge is up the spiral staircase that leads from the owner's stateroom to the base of the deck-stepped mizzen mast. Here, you can best enjoy the vessel while under way, with a commanding view from the exterior helm station across the roof of the enclosed wheelhouse. Controls for the five fore and aft sails are repeated here, as are the telegraphs for the twin, 600 hp V12 MTU diesels. Sail systems are fully automated, which allows the yacht to be operated by one person in most conditions, a long-held ambition of Fabio Perini's, fulfilled when he started to build the boats that bear his name.

Anyone who has enjoyed a stroll around the American Express New Zealand Cup Village will have noticed *Andromeda la Dea*, for she attracts some of the largest crowds. We are fortunate to have seen her in Auckland, and she will be with us for some time, as Simon Potter has promised her 'a

Andromeda la Dea is a favourite among those who appreciate timeless Italian styling.

OPPOSITE

Tom Perkins' *Andromeda la Dea* under a full press of sail with *Liberty* in pursuit.

huge, and well-earned refit after 10 years' incredible service'. Our maritime industries are lucky as well, for the work may take up to a year, and cost several million dollars.

Andromeda will receive carbon fibre in-boom furling systems from Marten Marine and her new wardrobe will feature fully battened main and mizzen sails, each with a more pronounced roach for improved performance. Carbon foils and bearings on foresail, staysail and fisherman will further contribute to a general update of Perini Navi sailing systems, which will include new winches from the Viareggio yard. Cosmetically, her steel hull and aluminium superstructure will be completely resprayed, and her brightwork refinished. The fabric of her interior will also benefit from some rejuvenation in the form of new carpets, and the regilding of some fine Italian fittings.

Her odyssey will continue in early 2001. Team New Zealand's successful defence of the America's Cup may influence her itinerary, for, like many yachtsmen, Tom Perkins may want to return to these shores for the next series, which is scheduled to start in October 2002. She might explore the coast of Thailand, or the pristine cruising grounds of Myanmar. But sail she will, for that is what this beauty was born to do. And, as Perseus did for her namesake, Simon Potter will continue to save *Andromeda la Dea* from the advances of savage sea monsters.

Specifications

LOA	47 m (154 ft 2 in.)
LWL	35.41 m (116 ft 2 in.)
Beam	9.2 m (30 ft 2 in.)
Draught (keel up)	3.35 m (11 ft)
Draught (keel down)	7 m (23 ft)
Max displacement	365 tonnes
Sail area	1000 sq.m (10,764 sq.ft)
Main mast height	42.40 m (139 ft)
Mizzen mast height	35 m (114 ft 10 in.)
Engines	2 x 600 hp MTU V12 183TC91
Generators	2 x 75 kw, 1 x 50 kw Northern Light
Fuel	41,000 L
Speed under power	13.5 knots
Range @ 13 knots	3000 n.m.
Construction	Steel hull, aluminium superstructure
Classification	ABS Malta Cross +A1
Naval architects	Perini Navi, Viareggio
Builder/Year	Perini Navi, Viareggio, 1990

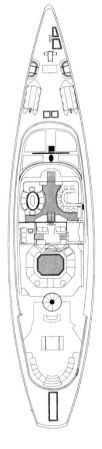

Andromeda la Dea

Double Haven

An exceptional creation

Henk de Vries III remembers the day that he learned of the project. 'It was mid-November 1990 when a very impressive parcel of paper arrived on my desk in the form of a bid package. None of us here had ever seen anything like it. There was a complete bundle, including construction drawings from the naval architects, in-depth reports on the tank-tested hull and on the ship in the water. There was a complete package on the interior design, more detailed than we had on boats that we were in the process of building. Glade Johnson had created a system of numbers, which broke down into other numbers, which pointed to material specifications, which pointed to suppliers: it was quite incredible.'

From a member of one of the founding families of the Feadship consortium, this was high praise indeed. But from the moment that her owner first contemplated the creation of Double Haven, she was destined to be something quite exceptional.

The search for solutions began in May 1987. The yacht had to accommodate 12 to 14 guests, and a similar number of crew, and the latter should be able to operate the vessel without disturbing the former. The owner's suite was to occupy the forward section of the upper deck, without jeopardising the visibility and functionality of the raised bridge deck. As Captain Nick Spence observed, 'If I was spending this sort of money, I would want the penthouse.' As a long-range, ocean-going vessel it should have reasonable draught and payload. A tender that could provide overnight accommodation for a small party should be carried aboard. It would have to be around 9 m in length, and should have standing room inside, so would be difficult to stow. Outdoor areas should be shaded when required, as the yacht would be spending much of its life in the tropics. The requirements for noise were quite simple: there should be none.

Nick Spence recalls the next few months as follows. 'Between May and September 1987, we had generated so many ideas, which, in turn, raised many problems, that we knew it was time to sort reality from dreams.' A meeting with the late Gerhard Gilgenast, a leader in contemporary yacht design, would go some way to solving the problems. Nick remembers that Gerhard's design work on the light displacement, 47.6 m *Azzurra*, being built by CRN in Italy, served as an interesting working example of the owner's deck concept. It would also provide him with useful information in advance of a trip to Europe in May 1988, during which he would visit a number of shipyards specialising in vessels over 30 m in length. His mission was to identify and clarify the type of problems both builders and clients experienced while working with outside designers.

However, it had become clear that Gerhard Gilgenast's over-committed schedule prevented him from providing the detail required. The French designer Richard Hein was retained in October 1988 to develop the conceptual design, demonstrate its feasibility, and prepare a detailed bid package. As Richard got to work, Nick set off on another series of visits to Australia, Europe, and the United States to refine the list of potential builders, and meet with the key subcontractors. By May 1989 Richard Hein had completed the conceptual design and preliminary set of specifications. Frank Mulder would assist with structural engineering and hull design of both an aluminium and steel version. Willem Van Capellan started working to minimise noise and vibration, while Heinen & Hopman set about engineering the air conditioning system. The following month, Glade Johnson's proposal was accepted ahead of those submitted by three other competing interior designers.

A model of the aluminium hull version was successfully tank tested in Vienna during December, but tank tests of a dry docking recovery system for the large tender proved inconclusive. The project was gathering momentum, and by May 1990, Richard Hein's group had completed their work, and Glade Johnson had completed a masterpiece of detail and documentation for an incredible interior. There were still a few undecided issues, so Nick sought an independent assessment from a firm of expert marine engineers based in Seattle. This study highlighted a number of minor problems. The engine room needed to be a bit bigger, and the aluminium hull version was probably too shallow for the required payload. As Nick put it, 'While we did not have all the answers, three years of hard work gave the shipyards a lot to study, and with recession affecting their order books, the timing was too good. We had to go ahead.'

Richard Hein and Glade Johnson put the final documents together as a package with the float-in tender and the existing hull and engine room designs. Meanwhile, Henk de Vries was engaged in a campaign to get his family's name firmly fixed in the client's mind. He had drawn up a long list of questions, and would send five each day. He prepared a quotation, outlining what the yard proposed to build, along with the price and a payment schedule. This included several pages of remarks about areas that needed further investigation. He was thanked for delivering the documents in good time, but was reminded that none of the bids would be examined until the end of February.

By April 1991, there were three contenders left in the running, two of whom were Dutch. 'The unusually long time spent in these negotiations was partly dictated by the complexity of the vessel, and partly by Captain Spence's phenomenal attention to detail,' recalls Henk de Vries. By the middle of June there were only two yards left in contention, and after several more days of intense negotiations, there was one, and a Letter of Intent was signed. Henk recalls the occasion: 'It was a great day for de Vries and Feadship. We still had to formally sign the contract — that took place in July 1991 — but at that moment we knew we were about to build one of the most sophisticated, complicated and unique super yachts ever to have been constructed.'

The design would be refined by Frits de Voogt, and the subsequent build undertaken by technical director Johan De Vries and the hundreds of craftsmen at the de Vries yard.

The aluminium superstructure would be built at Jachtwerf Gouwerok, one of the oldest shipyards in the Netherlands. The whole story is faithfully documented by Howard Finger in his excellent book *Double Haven*, as is an account of the launch on 30 August 1993, over six years after her owner and captain had started work on the project.

Of the motor yachts seen in the South Pacific, *Double Haven* is arguably the most memorable. Her physical presence seems greater than her 51 m length, but her sculptured profile keeps her impressive superstructure in balance with her relatively low freeboard. Viewed from forward, the thrust of her bow is enhanced by the reverse sheer that envelops her main deck, and the streamlined contours of the bridge and the owner's accommodation. Seen from either side, the diagonal lines that sweep upward from the foredeck resemble wings, tipped at their upper extremities by the linear texture of the air intakes. Similarly styled fashion plates at main deck level lend lightness to the way the vessel carries her two upper decks, and this is accentuated by the styling of the side windows. Her stern sections are lofty, but their height is disguised by the treatment of the after extremities of the decks. And her masts are further examples of the sculptor's art, and a tribute to Jan Maarsen who retired after 50 years' service to De Vries once he had finished them.

You board *Double Haven* over the full-width transom gate that allows the principal tender, *Double Happiness*, to be lowered over the stern with the Akerboom crane jibs built into the deck head. Ahead is a central staircase, between the two doors that lead to the water sports room and dive centre to port, and the workshop and engine room to starboard. At the top of the stairs, glass doors open automatically to reveal the after lounge. This is a bright and comfortable area, decorated in pastel colours, and featuring sycamore and bird's eye maple furniture. George Kalogridis worked closely with Glade and Pennie Johnson to create the carpets here, and throughout the yacht. Fior de Pesco marble is also used on some floors as well as on countertops.

Moving forward, the main lounge has a more formal feel, and benefits from wonderful views through the large windows to either side. An aft-facing sofa curls around a centrally situated table, while, further forward, the dining table, made of sycamore and bird's eye maple, can accommodate 12 guests. A Chinese lacquered screen on the forward wall opens into the pantry, while the marble counter below can be extended to form a buffet. Incredibly, this versatile area can also be converted into a movie theatre or a discotheque, as the sofa can be divided, and moved aside to reveal an illuminated marble dance floor!

Forward and to starboard is a foyer, from where you can reach the lower guest staterooms via a spiral staircase, or the upper deck and the sundeck by way of more stairs aft of the main entry door. Further doors in the forward bulkhead lead to a day head to port, and a small dining room to starboard, which features an outward-facing, semi-circular settee and breakfast table.

Moving forward again, and up a short

Double Haven and her principal tender, *Double Happiness*.

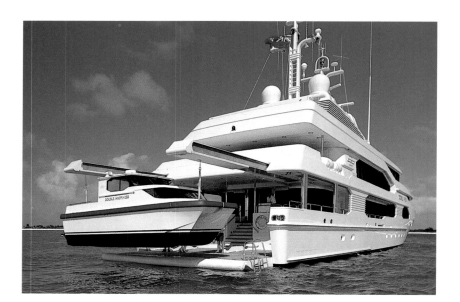

stairway, you skirt another marbled cloakroom, and the entrance to the captain's area which consists of an office, bedroom and bathroom. Another step up takes you onto the bridge, which affords the watch a 220-degree view of the surroundings. Radar and sonar screens, alarms and video monitors, along with navigation and communications systems are arranged in quadrants to each side of the captain's chair, and the small, centrally located wheel. A semi-circular sofa with a table on a raised platform, set into the after bulkhead, enables guests to watch the deck officers at work.

To either side of the wheelhouse are two exterior control stations, and beyond the Portuguese bridge, on each side of the foredeck, there are two seating areas for the use of the crew, a considerate touch that is in keeping with the philosophy of this yacht. The comfortable crew accommodation is situated below the foredeck, and this includes five double bunked cabins, each with an adjoining shower room, as well as a large dining area. A further, lower deck contains commercial laundry equipment, fridges and deep freezes, and enough dry goods storage to sustain the vessel for up to six months at sea.

Back in the midships foyer, you take the spiral staircase down to the guest quarters. Two staterooms, named Orchid and Magnolia, are configured as doubles, the Lotus room has twin berths, and Gardenia is designed as a stateroom or gymnasium and health spa.

The sumptuous surroundings of the owner's bathroom.

Double Haven's remarkable profile: the owner's stateroom is situated above the wheelhouse.

These generously appointed cabins benefit from natural light, as well as backlit shoji screens, and are decorated in variations of the pastel shades found elsewhere in the accommodation. Bathrooms are furnished with an exquisite mixture of marbles, and the gymnasium is also equipped with a steam bath and sauna.

Ascending the spiral staircase once again, you reach a small landing. Aft is the upper deck lounge, and forward lies the owner's stateroom. The central feature of this area is a large bed, but your first reaction will be to admire the panoramic view which, like the bridge below, takes in a full 220 degrees. A door on the centre line forward takes you out to the owner's sundeck, a semi-circular area recessed into the wheelhouse roof. The stateroom furniture is of maple and sycamore, and the fabrics are mostly silk, including the ceiling decoration. Moving to port around the stateroom bed with its large TV concealed in a cabinet at the foot, you enter the dressing room and bathroom. Facing aft, you will see an etched glass wall to your right, which conceals the heads. Steps lead down and further aft to the bathroom, which is decorated in rose-peach marble, heated to body temperature underfoot. The circular shower, whirlpool bath, and twin basins are also finished with marble, accented by stainless steel and gold fittings. A further head and shower is situated aft, and to starboard, and this can be accessed from the landing at the top of the stairway leading up from the foyer.

The midships section of the upper deck contains a lounge, with entertainment centre and a full range of office equipment including a fold-out desk. A sofa to port can be converted into a king-sized bed for extra guests, and a small table is situated to starboard along with four chairs. Large windows to either side afford superb views. A kitchen has been installed in the after section of the lounge, and this also serves the upper aft deck, which is reached through double doors. Here you will find an L shaped settee to starboard, and a circular table to port where 12 guests can enjoy dinner. The after end of the deck is raised, and acts as a comfortable sun pad.

Moving up the stairs towards the flying bridge, you will emerge through an electrically operated skylight onto the sundeck. Aft of you, the yacht's second tender, the 5.3 m *Double Harmony*, sits on her chocks, ready to be craned into the sea. A whirlpool, offering fresh or salt water bathing, is installed amidships between the arched mast supports and the air intakes, or 'wingtips', to either side. Further forward are two tables, bracketed by sofas, which form the octagonal shape that is carried through much of the accommodation. These can be moved to allow extra space for cocktails or dancing. And forward again, just abaft the helicopter pad above the owner's accommodation, are the external bridge controls.

Standing at the wheel, you reflect upon everything you have seen, and you think about all the people who came together over a period of more than six years that it took to create this superlative yacht. She has sailed for more than seven years now, and will shortly complete a total of sea miles equivalent to three circumnavigations. She knows the cruising grounds of the Mediterranean and the Caribbean, but she has also seen Alaska, Japan, and some of the remotest atolls in Micronesia. Practice made this exceptional creation perfect, along with tireless research, and a healthy measure of patience.

Specifications

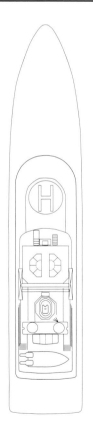 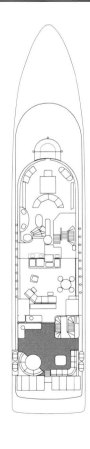  

51 m (167 ft 4 in.)	**LOA**
45.5 m (149 ft 3 in.)	**LWL**
9.3 m (30 ft 6 in.)	**Beam**
3.45 m (11 ft 4 in.)	**Draught**
773 tons	**Displacement (loaded)**
16 knots	**Speed (maximum)**
14 knots	**(cruise)**
2 x Caterpillar 3512 DI-TA, 1430 bhp @ 1600 rpm	**Engines**
3 x 125 kw Northern Lights	**Generators**
Vosper Thornycroft	**Stabilisers**
128,000 L	**Fuel**
Steel hull, aluminium superstructure	**Construction**
+100A1 PC Yacht, LMC-UMC	**Classification**
Richard Hein, Frits de Voogt	**Naval architects**
Glade Johnson	**Interior design**
De Vries Scheepsbouw, 1993	**Builder/Year**

Hetairos

A good companion

There is something reassuring about the word companion; it suggests friendliness and loyalty, comradeship and dependability. It has nautical overtones as well; a companion is an older term for a raised frame on the quarterdeck, and the companionway leads to a ship's accommodation. Hetairos *means companion in Greek, and this yacht has lived up to her name during the course of 102,000 n.m. of sailing since her launch in 1993 from the Lemwerder yard of Abeking and Rasmussen in Germany. Her captain, Brent Daw, will tell you that the owner had her built so that he could enjoy some exciting new places with his family and friends. And he certainly has, voyaging from Alaska to Antarctica and from the Mediterranean to the outer reefs of Fiji. But it is not just her itinerary that makes the current* Hetairos *so remarkable, for she is made of mahogany and teak, and while these traditional materials complement her classic appearance, she is in other respects a thoroughly modern yacht.*

Experience and research are two of the principal ingredients for the creation of an outstanding yacht, and *Hetairos* is no exception. Four years of development resulted in a project that brought the owner's representative Jens Cornelsen together with naval architect Bruce King, and interior designer Andrew Winch. When Abeking & Rasmussen were asked to build *Hetairos*, her noble pedigree was complete. Her hull would be made from six layers of mahogany, using the WEST epoxy system, with four diagonal skins sandwiched by two longitudinal layers. This would then be sheathed with an outer coating of fibreglass to create an immensely strong composite with lower maintenance properties. Frames, stringers, and deck beams would be laminated, while the deckhouse would be built of teak with a mahogany interior. The deck and cockpit furniture would be made of teak with varnished coamings and vertical surfaces. The yacht's massive scantlings are evident from the plans; her keelson would be finished in three sections, with the middle part incorporating the bronze centreboard casing, and the engine would be mounted on a stainless steel base. With the exception of these two fittings, the structure is entirely wooden. Construction began during the northern hemisphere summer of 1991, and was completed in the spring of 1993.

Brent Daw joined *Hetairos* as her building engineer towards the end of 1992, and took command the following September. He sailed her to New Zealand, his homeland, via the Caribbean, Panama, Tahiti, Samoa and the Cook Islands, arriving in late 1993. More than a year's world cruising would ensue before she left Alaska for Antarctica by way of Vancouver, San Francisco, the Galapagos, Puerto Montt and Cape Horn. She was back in the Caribbean for the Antigua Classic Regatta in April 1996, having sailed up the eastern coast of South America, and she went on to contest the Nantucket Bucket in the summer of that year. Brent then took her across the Atlantic to Ireland and on to Germany for a winter refit at Abeking & Rasmussen. She cruised the Baltic during the following spring, before making her way to the Mediterranean for the summer, and left the Côte d'Azur for the Indian Ocean after the autumn regattas at Cannes and St Tropez. Another year was spent between the Seychelles, the Maldives and Thailand before Brent shaped a course for Auckland and the America's Cup.

Had you been in Auckland on the afternoon of 17 February 2000, you would have seen *Hetairos* lead the super yacht fleet back from Kawau Island to win the second leg of the New Zealand Millennium Cup. The loft and rake of her Southern Spars rig is immediately apparent, for her carbon fibre masts measure 42 m and 33 m respectively. These are cream coloured, as are her Vectran sails, which were made by Hood's Lymington loft, and all look well with her extensive brightwork, and the jet black span of her hull. The aggressive profile of her clipper bow is highlighted by the scrollwork at the forward end of her gold cove stripe, which sweeps aft from the base of her bowsprit to the long overhang of her counter and the gilded detail of her transom. Look closer, and you can admire the detail of the deckhouse with its attractively arched windows, and the skylights topped with stainless steel dorade ventilators. These accessories complement her timeless lines, but you will also see evidence of her power in the shape of the big Lewmar winch drums that surround her cockpit. For Bruce King has created a yacht of antique appearance with advanced systems, and *Hetairos* can comfortably manage 265 n.m. per day on passage, and has achieved over 300 on occasions. She benefits from shoal draught of 3 m, which enables her to explore areas normally out of bounds to larger sailing yachts, but with her six tonne bronze centreboard lowered for passage making, she draws almost 9 m, and sails accordingly.

Boarding over *Hetairos*'s graceful stern, you step across the coaming and down into a deep, oval cockpit. The after section of this well contains the 2 m diameter wooden wheel, with banks of instruments arranged to either side. The forward part of the cockpit accommodates an attractive table, around which guests can gather while the yacht is under way. Between here and the mizzen, abaft the deckhouse, is a shallower cockpit, with one of Bruce King's signature skylights in the middle. A table and chairs can be arranged here for 'al fresco' dining when the yacht is at anchor or in port. These two cockpits can be shaded with a rigid awning, which may be left up while sailing. Forward of the deckhouse are more skylights and numerous ventilators, which allow those below a good draught of sea breeze as an alternative to the air conditioning. A rigid inflatable tender and a pretty, clinker-built sailing dinghy sit side by side under the main boom, while another tender is stowed between the skylights on the foredeck. Two big Reckmann furlers, at either end of the bowsprit, control the staysail and the yankee respectively.

Moving aft, and down into the deckhouse through the door to starboard of the mizzen, you will find a raised table and elevated settees to port. The outward facing seating has a curved wooden back, featuring the dolphin device you may have noticed on the transom. This is an ideal place for breakfast in a new anchorage, as you can admire the surroundings through the arched windows to either side of the coachroof, most of which can be opened. To starboard lies the navigation and communications centre. This features an unusual chart table, which is more like a partner's desk in a law office. The table extends athwartships, and is supported at its inboard end by the flag locker. Two swivelling chairs are situated fore and aft. Radar and computer screens, wind instruments and engine gauges, along with GPS and radio equipment are built into the mahogany furniture under the deckhouse windows.

Aft of the navigatorium is the stairway leading down to the owner's accommodation, which extends across the full beam of the boat. A large double berth lies to port, while a desk and sofa occupy a similar position to starboard. Between them is a dressing table. The decagonal skylight, which you will have seen from the cockpit above, allows plenty of natural light and fresh air when opened. Head and shower are situated forward and to port, through the door at the foot of the bed.

Here, and in the main saloon, murals by the artist David Barker lend an airy and colourful ambience to the accommodation, which, along with the bright fabrics of the upholstery, provide a cool contrast to the heavy warmth of the mahogany furniture.

Back in the deckhouse, you can look down into the main saloon over the banisters to

each side of the central stairway that takes you down to this level. A massive beam spans the 8.4 m breadth of the saloon and dining area, and light streams down from another decagonal skylight situated amidships between the beam and the forward bulkhead. To starboard there is a wood-burning stove, and outboard of this sits a small bar, with seating in the corner behind it, from where the owner or his appointee can dispense drinks to the waiting guests. Across the saloon to port is the dining table, with a sofa built into the forward bulkhead, and several chairs bearing the letter H and the dolphin design you have seen elsewhere. A mahogany desk below a bookshelf, aft of the dining area, and adjacent to the engine room door, conceals an electric piano for the entertainment of the musically inclined.

The accommodation has a distinctly Edwardian feel, which is enhanced by the abundance of mahogany, and the visibility of the deck beams throughout the yacht. There is nothing unattractive about the framework of *Hetairos*, and no need to disguise the structure of the vessel as the designer would have to do had the yacht been made of metal or composite materials. But the fact that the deck above is just that, with no suspended ceiling, and that the full beam of the yacht can be employed, means that much artistry was called for to conceal the wiring and plumbing. Bruce King and Andrew Winch were more than equal to the challenge, however, with the result that the style of the interior is as ageless as the lines of the hull.

Leaving the saloon by the doorway in the forward bulkhead, you take a step up into the long companionway that divides the guest quarters. There are four cabins, two doubles forward, and two twins aft. All have their own heads and washbasins, and each double shares a shower with the twin on the same side. These cabins are decorated in a similar classical style, with mahogany furniture, and off-white panelling, with plenty of natural light from the prisms mounted in the deckhead.

Moving forward again, you enter the galley, which is situated to starboard, opposite the captain's quarters. This is cleverly configured for a cook at sea, with sinks and stove mounted outboard, and Corian work surfaces arranged in two L-shaped arms, fore and aft, with a small inboard entrance in between. The crew mess, and accommodation for the remainder of the ship's complement of five, is located further forward again, just shy of the fo'c'sle.

Back on deck, you reflect upon the amount that the crew has to do in order to keep *Hetairos* looking as good as she does. For this is a yacht of vintage character which has many miles to her credit. Applying one coat of varnish to all the vessel's brightwork takes 490 man-hours. Somewhere between six and 10 coats are applied each year. Because a lot her time is spent in remote areas, much of the mechanical maintenance is carried out by the crew, who make good use of the fully equipped workshop next to the engine room. But you would do no less for a good companion, and, in return, *Hetairos* has looked after her complement in some of the world's most distant waters. And she will do so for many years to come.

Specifications

38.25 m (125 ft 6 in.)	**LOA**
30.5 m (100 ft)	**LWL**
8.46 m (27 ft 8 in.)	**Beam**
3 m (9 ft 10 in.)	**Draught (keel up)**
8.7 m (28 ft 7 in.)	**(keel down)**
190 tonnes	**Displacement**
680 sq.m (7317 sq.ft)	**Sail area**
42 m (137 ft 9 in.)	**Mast height (main)**
33 m (108 ft 3 in.)	**(mizzen)**
MTU V12 12V183 TE 92, 980 bhp @ 2300 rpm	**Engine**
1 x 50 kw, 1 x 30 kw Northern Lights	**Generators**
10,000 L	**Fuel**
Mahogany and teak	**Construction**
Bruce King Yacht Design	**Naval architect**
Andrew Winch Designs	**Interior design**
Jens Cornelsen	**Owner's project manager**
Abeking & Rasmussen, 1993	**Builder/Year**

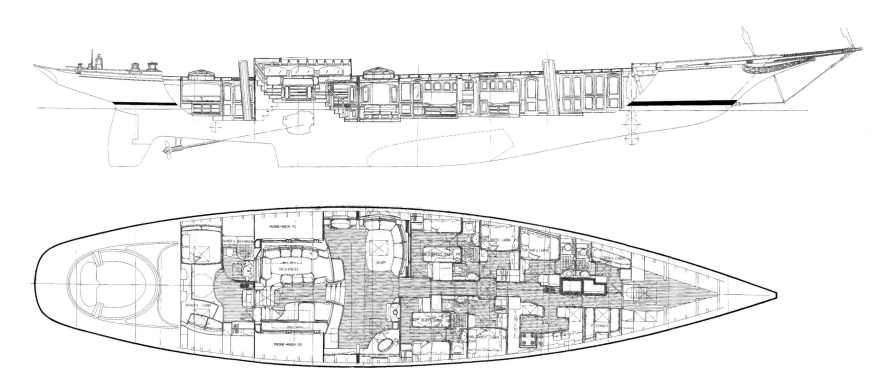

Hetairos

Yanneke Too

A yacht for all seasons

There is purpose in the lines of Yanneke Too, and in the loft of her rig, for she is doing what her owner intended when he asked Bill Dixon to design her. He wanted a good-looking yacht with a sporting feel and sufficiently shallow draught for the best anchorages in the world. As an experienced offshore yachtsman, he wanted her to sail fast, but to afford his family and friends the space and facilities of a motor yacht. He wanted her to be at home in all latitudes, to be a yacht for all seasons.

Of all the schooners designed by Charles E Nicholson last century, Margherita was probably the fastest. Built at Camper and Nicholsons in Gosport, and launched during the spring of 1913, she sailed to the Kiel Regatta in Germany and won five first prizes out of six starts, racing against Meteor, Germania, and Westward. On the penultimate day of the regatta, she carried away her fore topmast. The Kaiser, who owned Meteor, sportingly suggested that Margherita's captain, 'Shrimp' Embling, should select a new spar from the Kiel Dockyard, so that the yacht could race the following day. Her owner, Major Cecil Whitaker, accepted the gesture, and Margherita won again.

The First World War ended the era of the great racing schooner, and the 'Big Class' of the inter-war years saw the advent of the cutter. But Camper and Nicholsons had built schooners for cruising as well, and would continue to do so. *Sylvana*, built at Gosport in 1910, continues to serve her owners in the Mediterranean as *Orion*, and *Vira*, launched in 1927, and considered by many to be Charles E Nicholson's finest work, is best known as *Creole*. This famous yacht was enjoyed by the Niarchos family for many years, and is now owned by the daughters of the late Dr Mauricio Gucci. The latest exponent of this grand tradition, though, is *Yanneke Too*, launched at Camper and Nicholsons in Gosport during the English summer of 1995, and until recently in Auckland for the duration of the Challenger Series and America's Cup defence.

Yanneke Too's odyssey began with a passage to St Tropez, where she was much admired by all at La Nioulargue. She returned to Gosport, before sailing across the Atlantic to join her owner in Antigua for Race Week, and some local cruising. She then made her way across the Caribbean Sea, and passed through the Panama Canal, before exploring the western seaboard of Costa Rica and Mexico. Heading north, *Yanneke Too* paused in San Diego before continuing her voyage along the shores of California towards Puget Sound and Seattle. By July 1996, the yacht was in the remote and beautiful waters of Alaska, where she spent a happy month with her owner. Some heavy-weather sailing ensued during her return journey to San Diego, where she stayed from September until December, undergoing maintenance and modifications, after 15,000 n.m., and eight months at sea.

The New Year saw *Yanneke Too* tracking south past the familiar Central American coastline toward Panama. With her owner aboard, she headed for the idyllic waters of the Galapagos, where guests and crew explored this unique group of islands. Pressing on for New Zealand, the schooner visited the Marquesas, Tahiti, Tonga, and Fiji, before arriving in Auckland during August 1997 for a cosmetic refit at the Mount Wellington yard of McMullen & Wing.

Two months later the yacht headed for Phuket, via the Torres Straits, Bali and Singapore. Reunited with her owner, *Yanneke Too* spent the festive season sailing the Andaman Sea, the ship's company diving and fishing among the islands of Phi Phi Don, Phi Phi Leh, Krabi, and the Similan Group. She would go on to explore the eastern shores of Thailand, eventually reaching Koh Samui, 'Pride of the Gulf of Siam'. Later in the year, *Yanneke Too* returned to Bali, before turning back for Myanmar, and the pleasure of sharing Christmas with a Burmese pilot whose religious education had not prepared him for the appearance of Santa Claus!

Captain Charles Dwyer remembers the cruise around Myanmar as 'taking a step back in time'. *Yanneke Too* became one of the first super yachts to travel through this archipelago of undefiled islands, with their lush jungle foliage and white, sandy beaches. There had been talk of pirates, however, and a sinister-looking vessel approached the schooner one morning. Thankfully, the cutthroats turned out to be fishermen, wanting only to share their catch.

By the end of March 1999 they were headed for Singapore for a further period of maintenance, leaving in May to meet her owner in Cairns. She arrived, salty but unscathed, after 6000 n.m. on the wind, having paused only briefly in Bali and Thursday Island. After six weeks based in Hamilton Island, enjoying perfect sailing in the Whitsundays, she crossed the Tasman Sea, coming back to Auckland after almost two years.

Yanneke Too

Yanneke Too is a vessel of matchless pedigree, and the latest in a long line of schooners from a famous old yard. She has probably covered more miles in four years than some of her illustrious forebears did in 40.

Looking over the yacht, however, it is easy to forget how much sea time she has accumulated. Her powerful blue hull is pristine, and her teak decks almost rosy when seen against the cool white of her superstructure. Camper and Nicholsons built *Yanneke Too* from a cedar-cored composite, providing relatively low weight with strength and durability, not to mention high thermal insulation and reduced noise transmission. The helmsman enjoys tactile steering through twin wheels linked mechanically to a balanced rudder. Sheet handling is managed with traditional drum winches grouped around the after steering cockpit. Visibility is excellent, thanks to the low profile of the deckhouse, and the apparent absence of a tender, which is stowed in a garage under the after deck. Guests can enjoy the comfort of the large forward cockpit, surrounded by deep bulwarks, and protected by a folding dodger set into the deckhouse top.

The schooner rig traditionally offers relative ease of sail handling for a smaller crew, and the yacht's two 34 m masts, built in carbon fibre by Omohundro, are each fitted with Leisure Furl booms from Marten Marine of Pakuranga. North Diamond won the contract to provide the fore and aft sails, which are cut from Bainbridge cloth with UV-resistant Vectran inserts. Hoisting, furling and trimming operations are directed with a hand held control.

Yanneke Too's interior is the work of a talented troika, with Bill Dixon undertaking the structural design, Terence Disdale in charge of styling, and Richard Hornbacher contributing an aesthetic collection of fabrics and artwork. Going below, you will find a raised seating area to port, affording excellent views through the deckhouse windows. To starboard is the navigation and interior helm station, complete with a full range of instruments. Further forward, down the central companionway is the main saloon, with three sofas arranged around a table to port. To starboard, the bird's eye maple and briar dining table is bracketed by a white leather settee and upholstered wooden chairs. Colourful fabrics enhance the warm tones of the cherry wood panelling of the vertical surfaces and the quarter-sawn timbers underfoot. Clean, curving lines abound, punctuated here and there with items of exquisitely crafted

OPPOSITE

Guest quarters are bright, roomy and modern in appearance.

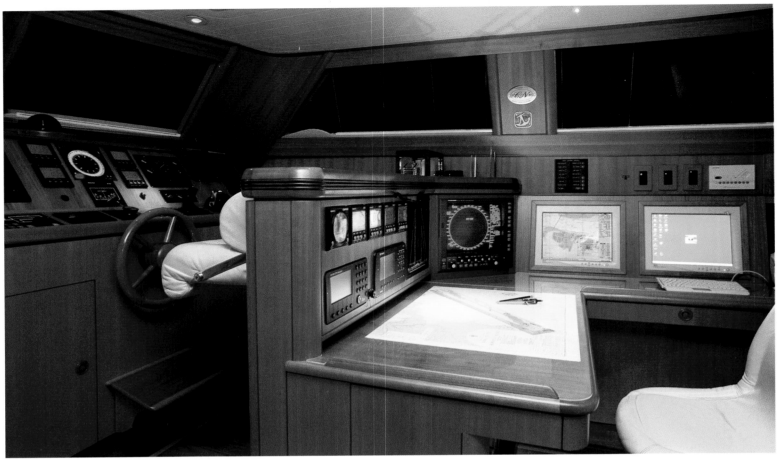

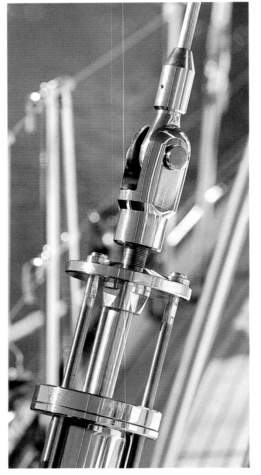

joinery. White headlining contributes to the contemporary, open plan atmosphere throughout the yacht.

The owner's party is accommodated in three cabins aft, which open from a central, cherry wood lined passage. The master stateroom fills the stern section forward of the dinghy garage, while a twin and a double of similar size are positioned further forward on either side. All are bright, roomy, and modern in appearance, with adjoining heads and showers. No concession has been made for the requirements of paying guests, as *Yanneke Too* is not for charter. Crew quarters for five, or six on passage, are situated forward of the saloon, past the galley, and consist of the captain's double and two further cabins.

Yanneke Too is a vessel of matchless pedigree, and the latest in a long line of schooners from a famous old yard. She has probably covered more miles in four years than some of her illustrious forebears did in 40. 'Shrimp' Embling would have given anything to sail around the world with Charlie Dwyer, who also has a background in offshore racers. And Major Cecil Whitaker would have felt quite at home, for *Yanneke Too* is most certainly a gentleman's yacht. What the Major would have made of America's Cup 2000 is another matter, however. He wouldn't have been able to get a new topmast overnight at any price.

OPPOSITE ABOVE
The navigation and interior helm stations.

OPPOSITE BELOW
An assortment of bespoke deck hardware aboard *Yanneke Too*.

BELOW
Carbon fibre masts by Omohundro.

Specifications

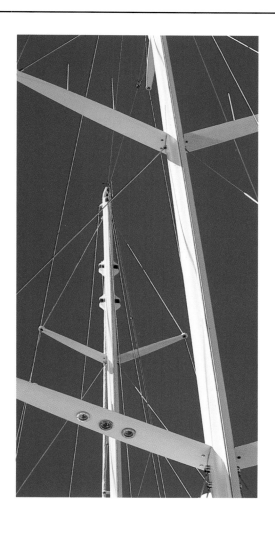

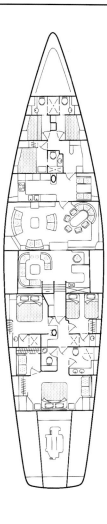

Value	Specification
35.43 m (116 ft 3 in.)	LOA
27.25 m (89 ft 5 in.)	LWL
7.94 m (26 ft)	Beam
2.9 m (9 ft 6 in.)	Draught
128 tonnes	Displacement (half load)
542.25 sq.m (5837 sq.ft)	Sail area (fore and aft)
North Diamond / Lucas	Sailmaker
Omohundro carbon fibre	Masts
Marten Marine	Booms
Lewmar	Winches
Lugger 470 hp	Engine
2 x 40 kw, 1 x 20 kw Northern Lights	Generators
11,000 L	Fuel
Composite	Construction
ABS	Classification
Bill Dixon	Naval architect
Terence Disdale	Styling consultant
Richard Hornbacher	Fabrics and artwork
Camper and Nicholsons, 1995	Builder/Year

Yanneke Too

Sapphire

Holland's glory

The Dutch have a long and distinguished maritime history, and a singular relationship with the sea. It has engulfed large tracts of their country on several occasions, and they have driven it back behind dykes, and set about reclaiming the areas of land they call polders. But generations of Dutch seafarers have worked with the North Sea and the oceans beyond in other capacities, as fishermen and traders, explorers and salvors, to name a few. And they have excelled in yachts; indeed we owe the word jacht in its original form to the Dutch.

Feadship, the First Export Association of Dutch Shipbuilders, and the generic name for the motor yachts built at the yards of de Vries and van Lent, has long been a benchmark for high quality. So have Royal Huisman and Vitters, whose sailing super yachts represent excellence in their turn. Another, newer name is Holland Jachtbouw, established in Zaandam during 1990 and now renowned for building remarkably fast traditional Dutch lemsteraak yachts, whose basic design comes from historic fishing craft.

Sapphire's owner, a Dutchman based in Amsterdam, is a keen and successful campaigner on the lemsteraak circuit. Towards the middle of the 1990s, he decided to build an ocean-going cutter with traditional lines and contemporary performance. He also wanted the vessel to succeed as a charter yacht, and engaged Andre Hoek to produce a design to be constructed at Holland Jachtbouw. The result was *Sapphire*, completed in October 1996.

Sapphire sailed from Holland on 10 October after a launching party held at the Ship Museum in Amsterdam. She sheltered from hurricane force winds in Falmouth before continuing her journey to the Canary Islands and Antigua for the annual charter show. It was soon clear that the owner's research would pay dividends, for *Sapphire* would charter for 120 days during her first Caribbean season. She spent the following summer on the north-eastern seaboard of the United States, showing an impressive turn of speed to finish second at the Nantucket Bucket super yacht regatta, before heading south for the West Indies via Annapolis, Charleston and Fort Lauderdale. A further 90 days of charter would be undertaken here during the northern hemisphere winter of 1997/98, before the yacht embarked for Palma de Mallorca and the western Mediterranean. A pleasant summer ensued, with *Sapphire* based around Corsica, before her captain, Andy Russell Smith, took her to Monaco and Cannes for the autumn round of classic regattas, following which she would cross the Atlantic once again for another busy season in the Caribbean.

During *Sapphire*'s West Indian sojourn she finished second in class to *Whitehawk* at the Antigua Classic Regatta, which also brought three of the four remaining 'J' Class cutters together for the first time. *Sapphire* sailed to the San Blas islands in the company of *Yanneke*, before moving through the Panama Canal and making for the Galapagos. By June 1999 she was in the Marquesas before heading for Tahiti and a month's stay in Marina Taina. A charter around Bora Bora was to follow, before Andy headed for New Zealand via Tonga and Fiji.

You may have seen *Sapphire* under sail in the Hauraki Gulf or the Bay of Islands and admired her sweet sheer and the clean sweep of her teak decks. Her hull is a deep blue, with the hint of a spoon bow, and a pretty, conventional transom. Topside, you will have noticed the classic line of her deckhouse, the varnished mahogany of her skylights, and the numerous dorade ventilators, which keep her spacious interior cool when the air conditioning system is not in use. Conventionally crafted cleats and handrails add to the period feel of the vessel. Aloft is a powerful, four-spreader Nirvana sloop rig, with Bruce Banks' sails. These and her spars are contemporary, as are the hydraulic Reckmann furlers which control the staysail and the yankee.

The after cockpit is elliptical in shape and features engine controls and a full range of Brookes and Gatehouse instruments forward, and to either side of the wooden wheel with its attractive, stainless steel binnacle.

The wooden wheel.

Guests can enjoy the roomy cockpit abaft the deckhouse, dining at the folding table, or watching the crew work the big Lewmar winch drums to either side while under way. The mainsheet traveller is situated towards the leading edge of the deckhouse roof, so the cockpit remains clear of sheet tails while cruising.

Entering the deckhouse, three steps down from the cockpit, you will find a chart table to starboard with a steering joystick, engine control repeaters, radar, automatic pilot, radio telephone, and a further bank of B & G instruments arranged along the outboard bulkhead below the windows. To port is a U-shaped settee and table, ideal for breakfast, drinks, or simply enjoying the surroundings. Headroom is generous, and the windows aft and to each side of the deckhouse can be lowered for a draught of sea air.

Several steps down from the forward end of the deckhouse, you will find yourself about to enter the saloon. But first, to port, is the galley, comprehensively equipped by Gaggenau and Miele, with twin steel sinks let into the partition that separates this area from the main body of the saloon. Aft of the galley is a passage leading to the crew accommodation, and access to the engine room. To

Specifications

LOA	30.5 m (100 ft)
LWL	22.59 m (74 ft 1 in.)
Beam	6.7 m (21 ft 11 in.)
Draught	3.4 m (11 ft 2 in.)
Displacement	95 tons
Sail area (main)	211 sq.m (2266 sq.ft)
(staysail)	100 sq.m (1074 sq.ft)
(yankee)	218 sq.m (2341 sq.ft)
(gennaker)	440 sq.m (4750 sq.ft)
Mast height	38 m (124 ft 8 in.)
Engine	Deutz 368 hp
Generators	2 x 34 kw Deutz
Fuel	10,300 L
Construction	Aluminium
Naval architect	Andre Hoek
Builder/Year	Holland Jachtbouw BV, Amsterdam, 1996

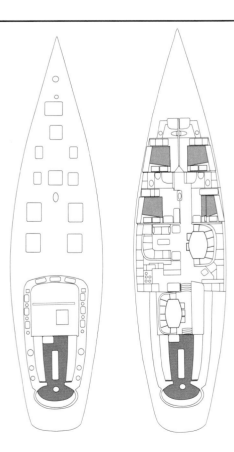

starboard, the captain's desk doubles as the navigator's station. Aft of this area is the captain's cabin.

The saloon itself seems extremely beamy, and features a settee to port which curls around an occasional table. The formal dining area is to starboard, and has a U-shaped sofa. White headlining throughout, complemented by honey-coloured maple floors and predominantly pale fabrics, accentuate the warmth of the mahogany joinery.

Moving forward along a companionway, which meanders around the mast, you will discover four cabins of similar size, but with differing characteristics. There are two cabins with double beds, each with pullman berths, along with another double, and a three-quarter-sized berth in the fourth cabin, which also features a pullman. Each has adjoining head and shower facilities, and all have mahogany furniture with white wooden panelling above. The traditional skylights above all the staterooms afford plenty of natural light.

It is sometimes difficult for the requirements of an owner to blend with the needs of charter guests, but aboard *Sapphire*, this has been comfortably achieved. Andy Russell Smith and his wife, Maggie, will hand the vessel and her crew over to Mark O'Reilly and Sharon Murphy, who will oversee a refit at Oram's yard in Westhaven before leaving New Zealand for a passage to Tahiti and the West Indies. Andy and Maggie will return to the Netherlands, for *Sapphire*'s owner has instructed Holland Jachtbouw to build a 46.3 m schooner to a design by Gerard Dijkstra for launching in July 2001. If *Sapphire* reminds you of the style of the great racing cutters of the 1930s, the new yacht will surely make you think of the schooners of the Edwardian era, some 100 years ago. And another glorious chapter will be added to Holland's maritime history.

OPPOSITE ABOVE

Sapphire's saloon makes the most of her generous beam.

OPPOSITE BELOW

The deckhouse table is ideal for breakfast or a light lunch under way.

BELOW

Sapphire's stylish sheer, seen from the port quarter.

Sapphire

Mari-Cha III

Fast company – the standard setter

Once in a while, a truly remarkable yacht is launched which sets standards of performance that redefine the capabilities of the industry. Robert Miller had owned big offshore racers before, and Mari-Cha III would be the latest in a series to bear this name. His idea was ambitious: to create a supremely comfortable sailing yacht that would be the fastest of her type and size in the world. She should be capable of establishing new records for ocean passages, but should also be able to cosset her guests while cruising. She had to be as light and stiff as possible to achieve her competitive objectives without compromising safety. And she would have an interior of unparalleled opulence, reminiscent of the great yachts of Edwardian England.

Miller instructed the French naval architect Philippe Briand to start work on the hull design and asked John Munford to produce drawings of the accommodation. No blueprint existed for a 45 m yacht that would surf downwind at over 30 knots.

Such a vessel would demand the very latest in composite technology along with a sound knowledge of racing rigs and systems. But avant-garde projects tend to attract the best minds, and by the time the build contract was awarded to Sensation Yachts in Auckland, 10 months of research and development had left nothing to chance.

The hull (actually constructed by Marten Marine) is of carbon Kevlar sandwich, and built to ABS scantlings. The interior furniture is an ingenious blend of Honduras mahogany veneer backed with lightweight Nomex, most of which can be dismantled and removed for racing, when pipe cots would be installed for those off watch. *Mari-Cha III* can carry 1750 gallons of water ballast for optimum upwind performance, and her fin keel and bulb weigh in at a whopping 41,000 kg.

On deck, her massive Lewmar winch drums are driven by HPS hydraulics while cruising, or by carbon fibre pedestals operated by her racing crew of 25 to comply with the rules of the World Speed Sailing Record Council. Aloft, her towering ketch rig, built from carbon composite by Auckland's Southern Spars, carries sails made by North and Voile Système Incidence. Riggarna and Aramid created her rod rigging, with huge Reckmann furlers controlling her headsails.

Mari-Cha III was launched during 1997 and completed by March of the following year. She made for Tahiti, following successful sea trials in the Hauraki Gulf, and a short cruise to the Bay of Islands. Robert Miller joined his yacht for a few days in French Polynesia, but *Mari-Cha III* was already in a hurry, pressing on for Panama and the north-eastern seaboard of the United States. Here, she won the annual Nantucket Bucket super yacht race before making for Newport, Rhode Island, to prepare for her Atlantic record attempt.

Jef d'Etiveaud had been *Mari-Cha*'s build captain, and he now set about making her ready for the trip with co-skipper André Luthy and their crew. During September, the team that would try to set the fastest time for the historic crossing from Sandy Hook to the Lizard began to assemble. Robert Miller joined his crew in New York, and all awaited the critical window of weather that would signal *Mari-Cha*'s departure.

The result was at once successful and spectacular. *Mari-Cha* crossed the finishing line off Britain's Cornish coast at 12.08.17 on 24 October 1998. She had made the crossing in a new record time of eight days, 23 hours, 59 minutes and 41 seconds at an incredible average speed of 14 knots. It was the crowning conclusion to a triumphant year, for *Mari-Cha III* had already won the 1997 Superyacht Society's award for the Best Sailing Yacht over 36 m LOA, as well as the prize for the Best Sailing Yacht Interior. But *Mari-Cha* would not rest on her laurels for long. After a short stay in southern England she made for the French port of La Rochelle, home of Philippe Briand and the Incidence sail loft, where she would remain for a month before setting sail for the West Indies.

The second Atlantic crossing from La Rochelle to Antigua was completed in a little over two weeks, and *Mari-Cha* arrived in Antigua on Christmas Day. She would return for Race Week after a sprint to Venezuela and the San Blas Islands, and would acquit herself well, in spite of an unfavourable rating. With her brief Caribbean season at an end, *Mari-Cha* set sail for the Mediterranean and Palma de Mallorca with a passage crew of nine. Her northern hemisphere summer itinerary would include racing with her owner and the King of Spain during September, and an appearance at the annual Monaco Boat Show.

André Luthy recalls the subsequent months as a series of fast passages punctuated by 'pit stops' during which the yacht would take on fresh provisions before setting off again. *Mari-Cha III* left Monaco at the beginning of October 1999 for Martinique, her

**Cockpit close-up: the weight of
the crew on the weather rail
may be augmented by internal
water ballast.**

fourth trans-Atlantic passage in 12 months. She was using the sails from her first,
record-breaking run, just as a new suit was being built for the Sydney to Hobart Race.
She reached Panama from Martinique in less than three days, and would arrive in Tahiti
a mere 16 days after leaving the Canal. The yacht arrived in Auckland on 16 December,
after a series of 340-mile days, to take on her third suit of sails, and made it to Sydney
with enough time to prepare for the race to Hobart. *Mari-Cha* was in a class of her own
in more ways than one, for her entry paved the way for the Super Yacht division that will
race in the 2001 event. And she set a benchmark time of 42 hours and 42 minutes for the
event, a new record.

But there was to be no rest for the giant ocean racer and her crew, for she was due
back in Auckland to witness the Louis Vuitton Cup finals, and the thirtieth America's
Cup defence. She contested the New Zealand Millennium Cup race to Kawau Island
and back during 16/17 February, which she won at a canter, bringing back the trophy
for Fastest Sailing Yacht.

You saw her on the way up to Kawau on the first day, scything through the chop off
Rangitoto on a close reach. Her sheer length is impressive enough, as is the sky-scraping
stature of her rig, but the aura of power is what stays with you long after she is gone. Her
lines are exceptionally clean, from the jut of her destroyer bow to the cambered slope of
her reverse transom. At sea she looks wantonly aggressive, but in a tranquil anchorage she
seems serene — a yacht that has nothing further to prove and is assured of her pedigree.

Sitting with André Luthy in the yacht's grand saloon, you may wonder aloud at *Mari-
Cha*'s competitive achievements. For you are relaxing on a luxurious sofa, surrounded by
mahogany panelling and furniture, paintings and old-fashioned light fittings. You can

hardly imagine pipe cots bolted to the bare hull, or the sea surging past the rectangular portholes at more than 20 knots. The very logistics of running such a vessel are mind-boggling, with containers moving around the world, and suits of sails being prepared in the southern hemisphere as the yacht is racing across the North Atlantic. The on-board sail wardrobe alone consists of four spinnakers, Code 0, 5 and 7, along with a genoa, blast reacher, blade, Number 3, staysail, main, mizzen, and mizzen staysail; clothing and provisions for 25 crew; well, the list goes on.

You may already have looked over the guest accommodation aft, and you could be forgiven for thinking that you were in a yacht from an earlier time and another drawing board. WC Storey or GL Watson might have designed the three staterooms off the companionway aft of the pilothouse, although some of the fittings have the feel of Fife. John Munford has created a timeless atmosphere with materials that are of vintage appearance while incorporating the best of contemporary composite technology.

The owner's suite can be reached through his study, or directly from the after deck by way of a hatch which reveals a curving mahogany stairway. The understated fabrics and soft furnishings serve only to accentuate the warmth of the wood, while the white deckhead creates an even greater feeling of space. A comfortable place, you may think, to be off watch in a howling Atlantic gale!

The study is further forward to starboard, while across to port is the owner's bathroom, trimmed with grey marble with accessories by Czech and Speake. Moving into the companionway, which leads to the pilothouse, you will find a twin cabin to starboard and a double to port. These are the same size, and are quite roomy, considering that the yacht's water ballast tanks are positioned between the outboard bulkhead and the hull.

Stepping up to the pilothouse, you are entering another world. Streamlined windows wrap around the structure, which slopes forward to blend into the coach roof. Visibility is good, and further windows are situated in the after bulkhead and the roof, so that the captain can keep an eye on sail trim while navigating. Raised settees are fitted to each side for guests to enjoy the action, as well as off-watch racing crew on stand-by. The navigator sits in a central seat of the type used in rally cars, with communication equipment to port. A range of engine and generator switches and gauges are situated to starboard, either side of the stairway leading down to the saloon. Because the two steering stations are positioned well forward in the cockpit, communications between navigator and helmsman are easy, with ready access to the deck through a door in the after bulkhead.

Moving forward through the saloon, you will reach the galley to port. This area is quite compact, a bonus when the yacht is moving fast, for everything is to hand, and meals for the large racing crew can be prepared at regular intervals. A full range of modern equipment also means that the cook has the wherewithal to produce more sumptuous and leisurely dinners for the owner's party when *Mari-Cha III* is in cruising mode. Three cabins with two bunks apiece are arranged between the galley and the crew mess, and each is equipped with head and shower. Further pipe cots are fitted to either side of the large fore peak, which also serves as a sail bin. Spare blocks and lengths of cordage are also kept in this area, which is separated from the crew quarters by a watertight door. While the guest staterooms are those of a super yacht, the fo'c'sle is most definitely that of a racing yacht, and it is here that you can see how the hugely strong hull has been built.

Having emerged from the sail bin onto the foredeck, you look aloft at the mighty masts, each with four sets of swept-back spreaders. And you are reminded of André's remark that 'you have to be careful with such big sails'. Racing apart, it is a testament to the seamanship of the passage crew that the only damage sustained during the long leg from Monaco to Auckland was one broken block. Standing on the bow, beside the powerful Reckmann furlers, you contemplate the broad expanse of the teak deck, the flush-fitting Rondal hatches, and the sail-handling hardware from Navtec, Harken and Frederiksen. Abaft the mainmast is the forward cockpit with six Lewmar winch drums and two carbon fibre pedestals. Forward of the mizzen is the steering cockpit, with a

Specifications

LOA	44.7 m (146 ft 8 in.)
LWL	38 m (124 ft 7 in.)
Beam	9 m (29 ft 6 in.)
Draught	4.5 m (14 ft 9 in.)
Displacement (cruising)	126,000 kg (277,200 pounds)
(racing)	110,000 kg (240,000 pounds)
Sail area (upwind)	1000 sq.m
(downwind)	1680 sq.m
Sailmakers	North & Voile Système/Incidence
Spars	Southern Spars (carbon composite)
Rigging	Rod, Riggarna & Aramid
Winches	Lewmar
Engine	Caterpillar 600 hp
Generators	40 kw Northern Lights, 15 kw Panda, 15 kw hydraulic generator
Fuel	9000 L
Construction	Carbon composite
Classification	ABS
Naval architect	Philippe Briand
Interior design	John Munford Design
Project manager	Jef d'Etiveaud
Hull construction	Marten Marine
Builder/Year	Sensation Yachts, 1996/97

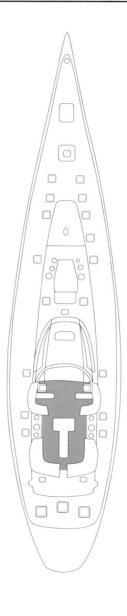

wheel and instrument console to either side. Between these consoles and the pilothouse are two armchairs. They face each other, with their backs to the rail, and are electrically adjustable to compensate for the angle of heel — the ultimate, perhaps, in cockpit comfort for an owner on a record-breaking run!

More Lewmar winches are sited to port and starboard, along with others clustered around the mizzen. The running backstays are led to further drums aft of the guest cockpit, which is below the mizzen boom. This area is remarkably free of the clutter that you associate with a racing yacht with sheet tails stowed in canvas bins, and settees built into the after perimeter of the coaming.

You leave *Mari-Cha* by taking a few steps down to the bathing platform, which hinges outward from the transom, and acts as the door to the tender garage in the stern. As you take a last look at the yacht from this angle it may occur to you that this is the view that her competitors have been getting used to as well!

A fast fetch into Auckland harbour.

Mari-Cha III

Charlatan

No pretender

Y ou can't help wondering how Charlatan came by such a name, for a charlatan pretends to be something he or she is not. This yacht is everything her owner intended, which is the latest and best in super yacht design, construction and technology. But he has owned Calculus and Consensus, as well as Catalyst, so it is fair to assume that the next one might be christened Consistency. For the creation of an ideal yacht, you need experience, and it is helpful if those involved have worked together before. And you don't stop thinking, or searching for ways in which an already superior vessel can be improved.

Captain Craig Roe will tell you that serious planning for the new yacht began aboard Catalyst during the northern hemisphere summer of 1996 in Maine. Every detail of the boat was re-examined by the owner, with input from the crew of four. Ron Holland, one of the world's most celebrated yacht designers, drew up plans for Charlatan, which was to be almost 6 m longer overall, and Tony Hambrook's team at Alloy Yachts started construction on 1 May 1997.

The bow fronted chest in the lower saloon.

Guests can enjoy panoramic views from the pilothouse.

The story of the owner's involvement with New Zealand goes back to 1993. Craig Roe and his American wife, Cassie, took over *Calculus* in Auckland during March of that year. This yacht, a 20 m Van Dam Nordia, built at Aalsmeer in Holland in 1982, had just emerged from a refit at the Auckland yard of McMullen & Wing. Craig and Cassie would take her to Fiji for the southern hemisphere winter, before returning to New Zealand and embarking for the west coast of the United States. From there she would go to the Caribbean, and up to New England. Considerable thought had already been given to her replacement and, having won the tender against international opposition, Alloy Yachts would build *Catalyst*, which was launched on 1 March 1995.

Craig and Cassie, together with Mike O'Reilly and Karen Smart, lost no time in taking their new charge to sea, and were soon cruising the east coast of Australia. From there they would make for South Africa, via the Cocos Islands, before sailing across the Atlantic to Antigua, where the yacht would be based for a busy 1995/96 charter season. Moving north to Maine for the summer, where her replacement would be discussed, *Catalyst* subsequently sailed south to the Fort Lauderdale Boat Show, and on to winter in West Indian waters. She was to be sold during the next few months, so Craig and his crew delivered her to Palma de Mallorca in May 1997, before flying back to New

Zealand to prepare for the launch of *Charlatan*.

The new yacht would measure almost 34 m LOA, and would displace almost 50 per cent more than her predecessor. While the bulk of the team that created *Catalyst* would be the same, there were some new players, notably Justin Redman and Mark Whitely, who would design *Charlatan*'s interior. At the owner's instructions, and in conjunction with project manager David Barwell, they arranged for a full-size plywood mock-up of the accommodation to be built in a warehouse on the Isle of Wight. This was a great success, for the owner could easily 'visit' the yacht in England, and get a feel for the way the interior would work. Videos were sent to the yard in New Zealand, and one of Alloy's own designers spent time on the Isle of Wight before finalising the build specification.

Alloy Yachts has an unblemished reputation for launching on time, and the boat would leave the yard during the course of October 1998 to undergo further commissioning work and sea trials. She would be handed over to her owner on 10 January 1999, and would enjoy a North Island cruise in company with *Savannah*, another Alloy Yacht, before sailing to French Polynesia for nearly five months with her owner's family and friends. She would return to Auckland's America's Cup Village in time to witness a summer of racing.

You may have seen her on the Hauraki Gulf, or in the Bay of Islands during this time and, if so, you would have admired her deep blue hull, with its golden cove stripe and white boot topping. She has a tall rig for a cruising ketch, and your first impression may have been one of understated power. Ron Holland has a knack of designing yachts with enduring good looks, and *Charlatan* is no exception. There is a timeless quality about her from the debonair rake of her bow to the sweep of her traditional transom, and you need to look aloft to remind yourself that this is a thoroughly contemporary vessel.

Her masts are made by Matrix from extruded aluminium, her vangs by Navtec, and her booms are built from carbon fibre by Marten Marine, whose Leisure Furl systems have set industry standards. Hood UK supplied a wardrobe which includes Vectran main and mizzen sails, yankee and staysail on Reckmann furlers, along with an MPS and mizzen staysail in blue, whose central star cut panels are highlighted in a striking combination of yellow and red. Her masts are stayed with discontinuous Navtec rod rigging, the 40 m main having four sets of straight spreaders, and the 33 m mizzen three sets of swept spreaders with a solitary jumper strut. *Charlatan*'s hull, deck and superstructure are of welded aluminium construction from alloy grade 5083 H321 plate, and grade 6061T6 extrusion. She has 32 tons of poured lead ballast in her shell keel, and her semi-balanced rudder is welded from grade 5083 aluminium alloy.

You board *Charlatan* via a short passerelle which bridges the gap between the dock and a hydraulically powered swim platform which forms part of her conventionally designed transom. The passerelle can also be located amidships, and showers are installed at each boarding point for guests who may have been bathing. Moving forward along the broad expanse of teak towards the pulpit, you will notice the 15 stainless steel, flush-fitting hatches that are made, like the portholes in the hull, to a design patented by Alloy Yachts. Below the pulpit with its little teak seat, and to each side of the prow, you will find the 136 kg stainless steel plough anchors, which are controlled by two hydraulically powered V6000 Simpson Lawrence windlasses. A further 75 kg Fortress type anchor is stowed in the forepeak. A total of 14 hydraulically operated Lewmar winches manage the sails, with two Alloy Yachts' captive winches for the main sheet and main halyard. These complete the inventory of deck hardware, along with blocks, cars, and traveller controls by Harken.

Looking back towards the stern the coach roof rises from just forward of the mainmast to encompass the pilothouse and the coamings that surround the three cockpits. The pilothouse is something of a Ron Holland trademark, and its low profile belies the generous headroom below. The bulwarks that encircle the deck are capped in varnished teak, as are the taffrails that top the cockpit coamings. The principal guest cockpit is situated just aft of the pilothouse and is rectangular, with seating to each side. A large table to port, and a smaller one to starboard, allow guests to dine outside, and these contain a fridge and stowage for glasses respectively. This area is protected by a canvas spray dodger, built into the pilothouse roof, when the yacht is at sea.

The steering cockpit lies a little further aft, with access from forward and from the decks to either side. The central helm station features a substantial pedestal, which supports a dished wheel. Instruments are mounted on top of the pedestal, with sailing, throttle and thruster controls contained within the circumference of the wheel. The hydraulic steering system has a bypass valve designed to give the helmsman some 'feel', and can be switched to manual by way of wires connecting the wheel to a quadrant. A seat runs round the after perimeter of the cockpit with instrument pods located at each end. This cockpit is slightly elevated, and affords good all-round vision while sailing or manoeuvring.

The owner's cockpit is situated under the mizzen boom, and affords direct access to the master stateroom below. This area is also sheltered by a spray hood, and has seating all round with a small central table that may be lowered so that the whole area can become a comfortable sun pad. This is an ideal place to relax with a book and a drink after a lengthy trick at the helm! Two further teak seats are built into the corners of the pushpit further aft, from where you can admire the set of the sails.

You could also do this from the pilothouse, as the overhead hatches and nine fixed windows afford a panoramic view of the surroundings. The quality of the Redman and Whitely interior is breathtaking, with raised and fielded teak panelling offset by white painted deckheads with tongue and groove detail. Cabinets and joinery are also in teak, and the main doorways are arched with slender, fluted columns to each side. A blue sofa curves around the port side of the pilothouse, almost surrounding a coffee table, which can be electrically adjusted for height, and fitted with a larger top to cater for breakfast, lunch, or supper.

A handsome, outward-facing desk is built into the side of the pilothouse to starboard with drawers to either side, and this abuts a large cabinet to the right of the central stairway, which leads down to the lower saloon and dining area. The cabinet conceals a console, which contains a complete set of repeater controls and instruments. The console rises at the touch of a button, leaving enough room for chart work, and the owner or captain can navigate the yacht from this position while offshore in adverse weather conditions.

Moving forward, and down the central stairway, you arrive in the lower saloon. Straight ahead is an elegant, bow-fronted chest, to port of the entrance to the galley and crew quarters. This conceals a television which, like the instrument panel in the pilothouse, rises at the touch of a button. The port side of the saloon contains three sofas surrounding a table. To starboard is the dining table, inboard of a further sofa. Four beautifully crafted chairs are arranged opposite the sofa so that eight can dine in comfort. A fridge is built into a cabinet adjacent to the sofa, and this is positioned fore and aft, as are similar units aboard *Charlatan*. This arrangement prevents bottles falling out if the door is opened when the yacht is heeling over.

Open the door in the forward bulkhead, and you will find the crew mess. A U-shaped settee to starboard sits on top of two lockers that conceal the Miele washer and drier, and borders the table, which is finished in Avonite. This durable surface is to be found on the galley work surfaces to port, and in the shower rooms adjacent to the crew accommodation beyond. Galley equipment includes a gimballed Smeg gas oven, a ceramic hob, microwave and dishwasher, all by Miele, along with a trash compactor, and extensive fridge and freezer capacity. Crew quarters consist of two double cabins, one with an extra pullman berth, as well as a further bunk in the forepeak for additional passage crew.

Back in the pilothouse, just to port of the main companionway, you may have noticed the curving stairway that takes you down to the guest accommodation. Passing the door that leads forward to the engine room, you will find similar staterooms to either side. To port is a double, to starboard a twin, but the latter can be converted by sliding the inner bunk forward, moving the bedside table inboard, and easing the bunk back to form a double. Bright fabrics complement the honey colours of the furniture throughout the guest quarters. Shower rooms are panelled in teak as well, with vanity tops crafted from Napolean Tigre marble.

The owner's stateroom is situated at the after end of the passage, and is entered through a door that is both arched and concave in section. This detail is another delightful example

ABOVE

The stairway leading up from the guest accommodation.

BELOW

The raised and fielded panelling of the owner's suite is featured throughout the yacht.

Charlatan

This is a modern, ocean-going yacht with timeless good looks and an interior that is second to none.

OPPOSITE

Charlatan's **fully automated sailing controls allow her to be managed single-handed.**

BELOW

A windward passage.

of the superb design and craftsmanship found throughout the yacht. A bright blue sofa with colourful cushions is situated to starboard, just aft of the wardrobe and a chest of drawers. A further hanging locker is incorporated in the furniture to port. The double berth can be divided for sounder sleep when the yacht is heeling to windward. Another clue to the owner's seamanlike character is the Brookes and Gatehouse instrument panel built into the bedside table, which pops up on demand to display details of speed, wind direction and strength. And next to the painting on the forward bulkhead you will see a chromium clock and barometer made by Wempe, which is one pair of a number to be found aboard *Charlatan*. Through the door leading aft, you will find heads to port and a bathroom to starboard. This has a shower cabinet with a teak seat and footrest, another thoughtful touch for those wanting to freshen up after a spell on deck in a seaway.

This is a modern, ocean-going yacht with timeless good looks and an interior that is second to none. She was born of long, sea-going experience, drawn and crafted by some of the best in the business, and it shows. For whatever else *Charlatan* may be, she is certainly no pretender.

Specifications

LOA	33.94 m (110 ft 11 in.)
LWL	27.05 m (88 ft 8 in.)
Beam	7.6 m (25 ft)
Draught	3.4 m (11 ft 2 in.)
Displacement	125,700 kg (118 tons)
Sail area	620 sq.m (6675 sq.ft)
Mast height (main)	40 m (131 ft 2 in.)
(mizzen)	33 m (108 ft 3 in.)
Engine	MTU V8 183TE62
Generators	2 x 35 kw Northern Lights
Fuel	11,000 L
Construction	Aluminium
Naval architect	Ron Holland
Builder/Year	Alloy Yachts, 1997

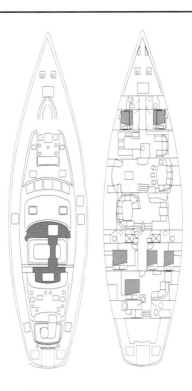

Liberty

Style, quality and the pursuit of technical perfection

Y ou may have seen some of the photographs taken of new Perini Navi yachts around the world, and enjoyed the sight of these powerful hulls under a vast spread of sail. Your eye will have followed the line of the leeward rail from the eminence of the bow, along the teak deck, past the bold curves of the superstructure to the broad bustle of the retrousse transom. You will have admired the soaring white masts and the set of the sails. But in one of the pictures of the 52 m ketch Liberty, you may have noticed something missing. There is nobody to be seen anywhere on deck.

Before you start thinking of the strange voyage of the *Marie Celeste*, remember that *Liberty* and her sister ships are among the most technically advanced yachts in the world. Sail handling is fully automated, and while you may not see the captain on the flying bridge, you can be sure that he is in the wheelhouse, and in full control. And this is what Fabio Perini intended when he established his company 15 years before *Liberty* left the Viareggio yard in 1997.

During the last decade, Perini Navi have delivered a series of evolutionary yachts with improved naval architecture, lighter spars with composite components aloft, covered tender wells, and automated platforms which afford direct entry into hulls with ever-higher topsides. Perhaps the most spectacular innovation aboard *Liberty*, built for a repeat client, is the unique midships 'sky lounge', set below the main boom. This affords guests the luxury of 'al fresco' dining with the benefit of an automatically controlled awning which can be raised by pressing a button should the rain come down, or should shade be sought from the midday sun.

But this is only one of *Liberty*'s many attractions as you will discover when you board over the wide reverse transom. The quarterdeck below the mizzen boom is almost circular in plan, bracketed aft by raised, teak-topped compartments which double as occasional seating. Forward, on the centre line, is a stairway leading up to the flying bridge, which features a full range of instruments, along with sailing and engine controls which are arranged across the coaming at the leading edge of this platform. Comfortable seating and sun pads surround the mizzen mast step beneath the bimini top, and guests can help themselves to refreshments from a large refrigerator. Back on the quarterdeck, to either side of a stainless steel rail, are steps leading down to the lower cockpit which is shaded by the aft overhang of the sea lounge roof. Large wicker armchairs and sofas with plump, striped cushions are arranged around a central table, just forward of the self-watering flower garden that is visible through the large glass panel between the stairways leading down from the quarterdeck.

Doors to port and starboard lead forward into the sea lounge or upper saloon. This area has some unusual features, including a central staircase with access from each side that takes you down to the after guest accommodation. The owner's desk is to starboard of the island created by the stairwell, a bar is situated to port, and the bookshelves here and in the after part of the saloon contribute to the comfortable, club-like atmosphere. There are sofas beneath the windows to each side, and big, easy chairs towards the middle of the sea lounge, which is panelled in American cherry. This attractive timber is to be found on the vertical surfaces throughout the accommodation, as well as on the soles of the guest cabins. Fabrics are predominantly blue and white, which add a cool touch to the warmth of the wooden floors and bulkheads.

The forward section of the sea lounge is also the wheelhouse. This consists of a full width control panel incorporating the latest electronic wizardry from Perini Navi, as well as radars with automatic plotting functions, sailing and systems computers, automatic pilot and engine controls. Guests can watch the proceedings from two elevated settees which are situated aft of the wheel, and to either side of the indoor stairway leading up to the flying bridge. To port is the captain's office, and to starboard is the chart table with related navigational and communications apparatus.

There are doors forward, and to each side of the bridge, and these lead to the sky lounge. You will find a dining table immediately in front of the wheelhouse windows,

The sky lounge may be shaded by an awning stowed in the compartment at the hub of this sunken circle.

RIGHT

The guest quarters benefit from natural light through large windows in the hull.

The relaxed ambience of the
sea lounge. The wheelhouse is
forward, beyond the stairwell.

which sits in the shade of the superstructure. Ahead is a sunken circle, three steps down
from the surrounding deck, with a tree-like, steel structure at its hub. This is mounted on
a chest, containing an awning, which blossoms from the tree at the touch of a button,
expanding to cover the sky lounge in the event of rain or strong sunshine. The awning is
attached to a number of pillars on the perimeter of the lounge, which themselves support
windows that emerge from slots in the surrounding deck should the wind freshen. Guests
can also enjoy pre-dinner drinks at three smaller tables, which are situated forward, and
to either side of the tree. A companionway leads down to the galley for ease of service.

Moving up onto the foredeck, you will notice the tender wells that conceal the two,
inboard-engined, Castoldi rigid inflatables which are the yacht's principal tenders. These
can be craned over the side and made ready for use about 10 minutes after the vessel has
anchored. Captain David Hutchinson has remarked that 'the yacht can change gear very
quickly', and you will remember this later when you leave *Liberty* via the boarding

platform in the port quarter of her hull. Fender stowage, and recesses for two life raft cases, are let into the foredeck to either side, and a teak seat built into the pulpit, past the two big headsail furlers, provides a splendid vantage point from which to admire the towering rig while the yacht is under way.

One deck below, the guest accommodation is divided by the main saloon and dining area. By day, the saloon benefits from plenty of natural light from the large oval windows let into the hull to either side. During the evening, wooden blinds can be lowered to cover these ports, and the cherry walls and teak floors positively glow in the soft lamplight. An eclectic range of ornaments contributes to the special character of the saloon, which is not unlike a drawing room in a colonial clubhouse. A grand staircase ascends to the sea lounge, while two doors in the forward bulkhead lead to the matching twin staterooms, and on to the galley and crew accommodation.

Moving forward again, you enter the galley to starboard, or the crew mess to port. The

The cherry walls and teak floors of the main saloon and dining area enhance the bright colours of the fabrics and soft furnishings.

former features black granite work surfaces and a range of equipment including an Angelopo stove and a steam convection oven for rapid food preparation. The latter is attractively decorated in cherry wood with blue upholstery. Crew accommodation is laid out forward of this area, and consists of one three-bunk cabin, two twins and a double for the captain. Each has an adjoining head and shower compartment which, like those in the guest quarters, are attractively trimmed with marble.

The after staterooms are accessed from the sea lounge. A double cabin is situated to either side of the central companionway that leads aft to the owner's suite, and both benefit from superb views through the windows in the hull that are found throughout the guest accommodation. In contrast to the flamboyance of the saloon, the sleeping quarters are decorated in an understated fashion, and you can fully appreciate the excellent quality of the joinery while enjoying the mixture of paintings, prints and other adornments chosen for the yacht. The owner's suite occupies the full beam of the vessel, and incorporates a double bedroom, dressing room, bathroom and study. Bathroom and dressing room are to starboard, the former offering a jacuzzi spa tub and a separate shower compartment lined with white Carrara marble, which also surrounds the bath and twin basins.

Moving aft through a watertight door, you enter a vast area of the stern that is much more than just a lazarette. There is a large door in the hull to port, which is hinged along its lower edge. This folds out to form a bathing deck and dinghy dock, complete with fenders and bollards. A roof-mounted crane jib slides out to retrieve water toys and the smaller of the yacht's rigid inflatable tenders, which can be stored in this stern compartment. An engineer's cabin and a small workshop are situated side by side in the capacious transom beyond the after bulkhead, while a sauna, shower and changing room are arranged forward of the dinghy platform. The convenience of this arrangement, along with the rapid deployment of the tenders stowed under the foredeck, means that this ocean-going yacht can be transformed into a mother ship for water sports in a matter of minutes.

Beyond the forward bulkhead and down the stairs lies the sub-deck. Two big Deutz diesels are situated behind removable panels with glass inspection screens to either side. Amidships, and to port, is the main control area of the ABS-rated, unmanned engine room. A central computer screen monitors all systems, logging valve, compressor and pump movements, and delivers several sheets of foolscap paper each morning to the chief engineer. The Northern Lights generators are nearby, along with the air conditioning plant, which changes the air once every five minutes throughout the accommodation. The programmable logic controls that manage the sails are located on the starboard side of the centreboard casing, and these are of proprietary Perini design with some GE Fanuc components. Further forward you will find the engineer's office, and then the laundry, dry goods store, refrigerator, freezer and wine cellar. The night generator lives in the forepeak beyond the Schottel bowthruster.

Style is a hallmark of the Perini fleet, quality is everywhere, and the engineering solutions developed during the life of the company are nothing short of breathtaking. Looking aft past the sky lounge along the broad teak decks at sunset, you can picture the glamorous parties that have taken place here. But glancing aloft, you remember that *Liberty* has sailed 50,000 n.m. in two years, and, having seen her at sea, you know she performs. She plays many roles, and excels in all of them.

Specifications

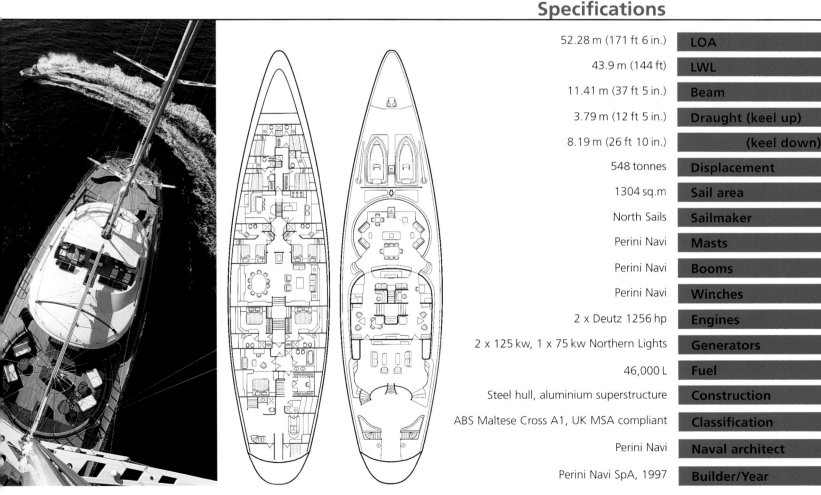

52.28 m (171 ft 6 in.)	**LOA**
43.9 m (144 ft)	**LWL**
11.41 m (37 ft 5 in.)	**Beam**
3.79 m (12 ft 5 in.)	**Draught (keel up)**
8.19 m (26 ft 10 in.)	**(keel down)**
548 tonnes	**Displacement**
1304 sq.m	**Sail area**
North Sails	**Sailmaker**
Perini Navi	**Masts**
Perini Navi	**Booms**
Perini Navi	**Winches**
2 x Deutz 1256 hp	**Engines**
2 x 125 kw, 1 x 75 kw Northern Lights	**Generators**
46,000 L	**Fuel**
Steel hull, aluminium superstructure	**Construction**
ABS Maltese Cross A1, UK MSA compliant	**Classification**
Perini Navi	**Naval architect**
Perini Navi SpA, 1997	**Builder/Year**

Freesia

The ideal discovery yacht

Discovery consists of seeing what everybody has seen, and thinking what nobody has thought.

ALBERT VON SZENT-GYORGYI (1893-1986)

Tender, funnel-shaped flowers are not what springs to mind when you first see the 36.88 m motor yacht Freesia. *Tough, you might think, or rugged. For she gives an immediate impression of seamanlike competence, and utter dependability. And that is what her owner wanted when he approached Dick Boon of naval architects Vripack International, and the respected Hakvoort Shipyard, both in Holland. The fact that his wife's favourite flower is the freesia was to determine the vessel's name, although naval historians might imagine otherwise. For* Freesia *was also the name of a 'Flower' Class corvette, one of the doughty Atlantic convoy escorts of the Second World War, which were immortalised in Nicholas Monsarrat's novel* The Cruel Sea.

Boon has over 7000 designs to his credit, and enjoys variety because, in his words, 'different projects make everybody think better, more creatively'. He was among the first to acknowledge the emergence of the 'discovery yacht', early examples of which had been converted from ocean-going tugs and trawlers, and the lines of *Freesia* are reminiscent of some research vessels.

The principle behind Boon's yachts of this type is to extract maximum efficiency from the hull without resorting to excessive horsepower and high fuel consumption. He therefore builds in aluminium, uses ballast tanks to maintain optimum trim, and arranges guest quarters so that minimal motion is experienced at sea. *Freesia* displaces 216 tons but, had she been built of steel, she would weigh 300 tons and require almost 50 per cent more power than that delivered by her twin 480 hp Caterpillar diesels. Her ship-like appearance also affords greater interior volume, both in terms of accommodation and the carriage of larger reserves of fuel than would otherwise be possible. Accordingly, she offers a range of 4500 n.m. at an economical cruising speed of 11 knots, and this distance could be doubled if her ballast tanks were filled with fuel instead of water. This makes her ideal for an owner who, as his captain puts it, 'is interested in going further afield'.

Looking at *Freesia* from the dock, you see a handsome vessel with a tangible sense of purpose from the height of her bow to the generous jut of her stern. Her expertly faired hull is finished in royal blue with a white boot topping to match her superstructure. A sturdy foremast is well stayed with rod rigging to enable the integral jib to lift her two substantial tenders over the side. These boats, a Boston Whaler Outrage and a Prestige

RIB, sit snugly on their cradles between the raised foredeck and the superstructure while *Freesia* is under way. The short stack abaft her wheelhouse supports a further mast, which carries radar and communications equipment on a series of staggered spreaders. This funnel is painted in house colours with three gold stars. A pretty, varnished dinghy, along with a life raft, is visible atop the upper saloon and this, along with a small inflatable, can be lowered into the water with a derrick.

Stepping onto the boarding platform, and moving through a door in the transom, you will find yourself on a broad expanse of teak deck, facing a large, walk-in lazarette where the owner's extensive range of fishing equipment is stored. To either side of this are short stairways leading from the cockpit where a substantial table provides comfortable 'al fresco' dining in the shelter of the upper deck extension. Doors to port and starboard lead forward into the main saloon, which features cherry panelling, sofas to either side beneath deep windows, with antique chairs arranged round a table in the middle. A cosy fireplace and bar flanking the entrance to the dining area add to the club-like ambience of the main deck.

There is extraordinary attention to detail in the more formal areas of the accommodation, and this is evident throughout the yacht. Virginia Freeman Rowan created this comfortable environment, which is complemented by the artwork collected by the owner specifically for this vessel.

The galley, also on the main deck, provides a workmanlike contrast to the saloon and dining areas with its stainless steel surfaces and commercial catering equipment. The chef enjoys a good view from here, which is a bonus not always enjoyed by sea-cooks whose quarters are sometimes set deeper down into the vessel. A small dinette area is set aside for the crew who may stop by for coffee and a snack during the course of their duties. There is extensive storage under the stairway outside the galley, and the volume of this area, along with the capacity of the fridge and freezer further forward, enables *Freesia* to cruise with a full complement for up to one month before re-provisioning.

Moving aloft from the main deck is the wheelhouse, along with a small pilot's cabin, and the upper saloon. The bridge offers near 360-degree vision through large windows, and those that overlook the bow slope forward in the fashion of a trawler. Again, you will be struck by the abundance of space in this area, which conveys the feeling of a small ship, but with the comfort and quality you associate with a yacht from a leading Dutch yard such as Hakvoort. Operating controls are arranged upon a central console, which is flanked by twin pilot chairs. Aft of this is the chart table, with a similar seat for the navigator, and a full range of communications and meteorological equipment. Occupying the port quarter of the wheelhouse is a table and a quarter-elliptical sofa where the owner and his guests can observe the proceedings while under way.

The pilot's cabin is down the stairs behind the bridge, and to port, beside the technical library and the entrance to a further, enclosed area beneath the wheelhouse which contains much of the vessel's electronic equipment. A day head serves the upper deck, and affords washing facilities for the pilot. Further aft, and to starboard, you will find the entrance to the upper saloon, a bright, relaxed area with settee, sofas and table. In addition to being able to admire the superb view, you can enjoy a variety of entertainment systems or, having helped yourself to a drink from the bar, you can step out onto the after deck to survey the surroundings.

Two storeys below, the owner's stateroom enjoys the full beam of the yacht and features two adjacent heads, one with a shower, and the other with a proper bathtub. An island at the foot of the double berth contains another entertainment system, and there is extensive storage space forward of this and to port. The owner's desk is situated to starboard between the bathroom doors. A central passage leads forward with guest accommodation to either side. This consists of three twin staterooms with adjoining heads, as well as a fourth cabin, which is presently configured as a gymnasium with steam shower. Forward of the guest quarters is the captain's cabin, along with the crew mess and berths for the engineer, bo'sun, chef, and the two stewardesses.

Freesia has made the most of the period between her launching in Monnickendam in January 1998 and her arrival in New Zealand towards the end of the following year. She sailed from Holland to the Balearics, before visiting Ireland and Scotland on her way back north to the Baltic for a summer cruise. Returning to the Mediterranean she would subsequently embark for the West Indies, moving on to Panama by way of the San Blas Islands in March of 1999, and then to Baja California and San Diego. Warranty work put paid to plans to spend July and August in Alaska, and *Freesia* eventually left Campbell's Shipyard for the Marquesas with the owner and three fishing friends aboard. A subsequent cruise through the Tuamotus brought the yacht to Tahiti by the end of September, where the owner's wife and four guests joined the yacht. *Freesia* subsequently shaped a course for Opua in New Zealand's Bay of Islands, where she would spend two weeks before heading for the Fiordland coast of the South Island, stopping at Bluff and the port of Invercargill.

Back in Auckland to witness the Challenger Series and the America's Cup defence, Andrew Johnstone discussed plans for the yacht following the conclusion of her sojourn

Specifications

LOA	36.88 m (121 ft)
LWL	33.22 m (109 ft)
Beam	8.18 m (26 ft 10 in.)
Draught	2.44 m (8 ft)
Displacement	216.65 tonnes
Speed (maximum)	14 knots
(cruise)	12.5 knots
Engines	2 x Caterpillar 3408C, 358 kw (480 bhp) @ 1800 rpm
Stabilisers	Koop Nautic Sea Rocq
Fuel	50,000 L
Construction	Welded aluminium alloy
Classification	ABS
Naval architect	Vripack Yachting
Interior layout	Vripack Yachting
Interior design	Virginia Freeman Rowan
Builder/Year	Hakvoort Shipyard BV, 1998

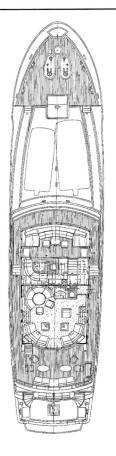
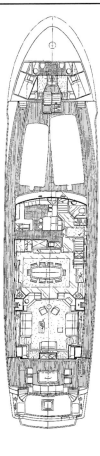

in New Zealand. *Freesia*'s owner is a keen outdoorsman 'who likes to take the vessel to places where there are no Super Yacht facilities'. Accordingly, she is scheduled to move on to Fiji and New Caledonia in April and May 2000, before making for the Whitsunday Islands and the Olympic Games in Sydney. Thereafter, her itinerary includes visits to Malaysia and Thailand, followed by the Seychelles, Maldives, and Andaman Islands. *Freesia* is due in Turkey early in April 2001, and will complete her circumnavigation with a trip to the Baltic for the northern hemisphere summer.

Freesia is something of an enigma, a yacht whose husky, if pristine, appearance conceals a beautifully crafted and comfortable interior. Her captain tells the story of a visit to Dusky Sound in Fiordland, west of Invercargill, where he came across some poachers busy fishing. The fishermen fled, having failed to notice *Freesia*'s gleaming topsides, teak decks and the American ensign flying at her stern. Later, having satisfied themselves that the vessel did not belong to the Ministry of Fisheries, they returned, and offered to sell their catch!

While *Freesia*'s rugged looks will always distinguish her from the super yacht fleet, there are other more practical benefits associated with this vessel's no-nonsense demeanour. She was designed for distant waters, and to be self-supporting for long periods of time. She may encounter people who, while used to shipping, might be hostile toward conventionally styled luxury yachts. So she should be safe, as well as seaworthy. Had he lived to see her, Albert von Szent-Gyorgyi might have been moved to change his mind. For *Freesia* will carry on discovering what few people have seen, while her owner continues to think what nobody else has thought.

A view from the bridge.

Freesia

Independence

Self-sufficient and sophisticated

The long cruises that this super yacht undertakes demonstrate the versatile nature of the craft, and allow her to live up to the name **Independence**. She is self-supporting in terms of provisions for about two weeks, which is remarkable for a sailing vessel that may have as many as 12 in the owner's party in addition to her permanent crew of 10. Any voyage into distant waters requires effective liaison with trusted agents, and all the local knowledge that the captain can bring to bear, for schedules must be arranged to include resupply by helicopter between visits to the larger islands along the way. Not that any hardship should be encountered with proper planning, for **Independence** has a cruising range of 4000 n.m. at 10 knots, and can make enough fresh water to fill her 12,800 litre reservoir every day.

In the last 18 years, Perini Navi has invested considerable time and resources in the development of yachts that combine the advantages of power and sail. This has been achieved by harnessing computer technology along with ideas developed by Fabio Perini's machinery manufacturing company, and applying both to the creation of a new generation of yachts that have consistently been at the forefront of the fleet. By the time Perini Navi delivers the 64 m, Ron Holland designed ketch that is presently in build, the yard will have launched some 30 distinctive vessels, and will, no doubt, have added to the present tally of nine design awards from the Superyacht Society, and *Show Boats International* magazine.

The 53 m *Independence* is the second of a series of hulls that began with her near sister *Liberty*. This class of large sailing yacht offers substantially greater accommodation than earlier models, not least because of the lower deck that runs the full length of the hull, where all the major machinery is installed. This means that guest quarters are completely unobstructed by the engine room, and allows the crew to move freely from one end of the

It is difficult to imagine how a big sailing yacht could be made any better, because *Independence* represents the state of the art.

OPPOSITE ABOVE

One of the guest staterooms, each of which is named for the DeVos family's favourite cruising grounds.

OPPOSITE BELOW LEFT

One of the six bathrooms in the guest quarters.

OPPOSITE BELOW RIGHT

The companionway leading to the owner's suite.

yacht to the other, without disturbing the owner's party. The increased hull volume naturally meant higher freeboard, but this is not apparent from outside, thanks to the dark blue topsides, and the relatively low profile of the white superstructure. The yacht carries her substantial beam well, thanks to extensive tank testing and wind tunnel work, and her contemporary underwater hull form gives her good speed under sail or power.

The list of Perini owners is something of a Who's Who of super yacht society, and this is not surprising, given the superior build quality and finish of the vessels, and their use of leading edge technology. Richard M DeVos and his family are seasoned sailors, and their current fleet includes the 51.2 m Feadship *Enterprise V*, and the 37.8 m Picchiotti ketch *Freedom*, along with an assortment of racing yachts and smaller craft. The owner's growing family prompted him to consider adding a larger sailing yacht to his collection, and, as a long-standing admirer of Fabio Perini's thinking, he bought the hull, which was to become *Independence*, after a visit to the Viareggio yard. She would be launched in October 1997.

Captain Kerry Piesch and his wife, Rose, had joined *Freedom* in 1995, after eight years in charge of the 30 m, Sparkman and Stephens designed cutter *Osprey*, which took them to many remote locations around the world. Their travels would continue, as they were

frequent visitors to Perini Navi during the course of the build, in addition to managing a full sailing itinerary for *Freedom*. In April 1998 *Independence* was handed over and visited Portofino, prior to embarking for the Amalfi coast via Sardinia. Following a short scheduled stop in the shipyard, she then moved to Greece and on to Turkey for an end of season cruise. Captain Piesch (known for many years as 'KP') would recall this with pleasure, as there were few other yachts about, and the 'Meltemi' wind was noticeable only by its absence.

Independence now headed towards the Caribbean for the northern hemisphere winter of 1998/99, ranging between Antigua and St Thomas with the owner's family and friends enjoying the new yacht. She visited Savannah, Georgia, before moving south toward the Panama Canal and the beginning of her first Pacific crossing. Once again, the family would make the most of *Independence* during the course of an itinerary that included 10 days in the Galapagos Islands, and a month in the Marquesas, spent visiting some of the more rugged and remote islands in the region. From there, *Independence* sailed for the Tuamoto Group, where the ship's company made good use of the extensive range of diving equipment aboard, while exploring the low lying atolls. Expeditions to Tahiti, Moorea, Bora Bora and Huahine followed, before KP shaped a course for Auckland via Tonga and Fiji.

You can board *Independence* over the stern, via the ladder which retracts into the starboard side, or through the large door in the vessel's port quarter. This forms part of the hull, and folds downwards to create a platform just above the waterline so that guests can board with ease from one of the yacht's 5.5 m Castoldi rigid inflatable tenders. Moving into the hull, you find the lazarette aft and to port, adjoining a small cabin, which

The big Perini ketches are among the most sophisticated yachts in the world.

is used by the security staff that sometimes travel with the owner. Tools, diving equipment and wetsuits are stored in adjacent lockers, and a jet-ski can be launched over the boarding platform using the sliding crane jib built into the ceiling. A head and shower can be used by guests after swimming, or by the occupants of the after cabin, and gym equipment is situated forward and to starboard, beside the door that leads through to the owner's quarters. Next to this door is the entrance to the engine room, and stairways to either side of the opening in the hull lead to the cockpit, or aft to the quarterdeck respectively.

Descending to the engine room, you pass between the massive banks of silencing equipment that serve the two 1256 hp Deutz diesels. These lie to either side as you approach the long centreboard casing that divides this area. The port route forward takes you through a clinically clean, white panelled passage, past the central computer that relays all the systems information to the engine room staff. Two of the three Northern Lights generators are located on this level, with a smaller version situated in the bow compartment. The workshop is to starboard at the forward end of the centreboard casing. Glancing aft, as you move towards the engineer's cabin, you think of the inside of a submarine, such is the concentration of equipment and instrumentation. Further forward again are the pantry, laundry, fridges, freezers and a dry goods store, and beyond these, in the forepeak, is the 75 kW Schottel bow thruster.

A custom-made
Perini Navi clew fitting.

Taking the forward stairway up to the lower deck brings you to the main galley, crew mess, captain's office and stateroom, and cabins for a further six crew. Teak panelling, along with white formica cover the vertical surfaces in this area, worktops in the galley are made of granite, and a comfortable settee in the crew mess provides seating for eight with folding chairs for the remainder of the crew.

Moving through the door at the after extremity of the crew quarters, you find yourself at the forward end of a long hallway which divides the guest accommodation. This is attractively finished in cherry wood with recessed and backlit mahogany hand rails, and white wool carpet conceals the teak and holly soles. The guest staterooms are named, and themed for the cruising grounds that the family has visited with the yacht. Forward and to starboard is the Fijian cabin, the largest of the staterooms, with a dressing room and bathroom, which has a tub. Further aft, and to either side of the hallway, are two twin-bedded cabins with extra pullman berths, called the Tahitian and the Caribbean. Each has an outward-facing desk, generous wardrobe space, and adjacent head and shower. Aft again, past the staircases that lead up to the saloon from either side, are the Grecian and Italian cabins, each equipped with double beds. Head and shower facilities are similar to those in the neighbouring staterooms.

The owner's suite occupies the full beam of the yacht at the after end of the lower deck, and is entered through a central lobby. To port is the stateroom, which offers an aft-facing, king-sized bed, and beyond this is a large bathroom with tub, shower, dressing table, and twin basins, surrounded with dusky-pink Rosa Portugala marble, which contrasts beautifully with the cherry joinery. The starboard half of the accommodation consists of a comfortable study.

The guest accommodation is remarkable for a number of reasons, not the least of which

Sheeting car and track.

is the abundance of natural light afforded by the large, oval windows, which are let into the hull in each stateroom. You can imagine contemplating a beautiful anchorage from the comfort of your bed as you make up your mind whether to take a tender or jet-ski out before breakfast, or to check your e-mail at the dedicated telephone point provided at each desk. Or you could move aft for a brisk workout in the gym that is located on the boat deck aft of the owner's suite.

Making your way back to the staircases in the hallway on the lower deck, you can take either to reach the saloon. Here you are reminded of the many precautions that have been taken to safeguard the owner's grandchildren, for there are concealed gates built into the furniture at the top of the stairs to each side. Facing aft, you are confronted by an inviting array of large sofas and chairs, placed around a central table. To port is a further sofa and easy chair, along with a writing desk, which is situated next to the door to the cockpit. To starboard, there is another cockpit door, and fitted furniture extends forward to the entrance to the dining room. Large, square windows provide a marvellous view to either side of the saloon, and the predominantly off-white upholstery is highlighted by the shades of red and gold in the carpet, cushions, and other fabrics. Looking forward towards the chest that divides the two stairways, you will notice the twin pillars that rise to the ceiling from the inboard banister rails. A large screen descends between the pillars and a projector from the deckhead further aft to provide cinema-quality entertainment. This is allied with a sophisticated digital sound system.

Forward and to starboard are the double doors to the dining room. The round table can seat up to 10. Another table, which serves a semi-circular sofa, is used for smaller gatherings or for the children at a family party. Leaving the dining room through the forward door to port you will find a well-equipped pantry, and a bar, which adjoins the saloon. Moving forward, past the day head, you reach the pilothouse.

While the yacht is normally controlled from the flying bridge when under way, this area allows a good view of the foredeck and the surrounding sea through the deep windows that encircle the forward superstructure. Instrumentation and computer screens, along with joysticks and controls for the sailing and engine systems are neatly arranged across a console in front of the centrally mounted wheel. Captain's chairs are positioned to either side of the main display, and a sofa is built into the after bulkhead to allow guests to watch the proceedings. The chart table is situated to starboard, and the captain's desk to port, next to the flush-fitting door that opens outward, and slides aft to allow access to the foredeck.

Moving towards the pulpit, you reach the two windlasses by the ship's bell forward of the breakwater. Turn around, and you will realise why the foredeck is free of any encumbrance. At the touch of a button, two large sections of teak deck to either side of the crew companionway hinge upwards and inboard to reveal the two 5.5 m Castoldi rigid keel inflatable tenders. These have 105 hp Yanmar inboard diesels and jet drives. Two smaller hatches, outboard of the tender wells, conceal the Quantum knuckle boom cranes that lift the tenders over the sides, and into the water. Further recesses enable inflated fenders to be stowed for ready use, and other hatches allow access to the emergency generator, water toys, and anchoring equipment.

Up on the flying bridge, the pilothouse controls and instrumentation are repeated on a console that extends across the forward coaming of the upper deck under the bimini top below the main boom. Helm stations are situated to port and starboard, and seating amidships allows guests to observe the computer managed sailing systems at work. All sails can be set, sheeted or reefed from here by working some switches and joysticks, and sails can be fully furled in little more than two minutes. You can fully appreciate the height of the powerful rig from here, and you may notice that the multiple, aerofoil section spreaders incorporate large slots to reduce weight aloft. Further settees and tables are arranged to either side of the after section of the flying bridge, around the mizzen mast step, and there is a small spa pool for those who want to relax while the vessel is under way.

The after cockpit is a relaxing place to discuss the day's adventures over drinks, and to enjoy dinner 'al fresco'. A large sofa and easy chairs surround the central table under the after superstructure extension, and an awning can be arranged to cover two further tables aft. These are positioned to either side of the centre line, and forward of a wide, crescent-shaped settee that follows the contour of the after cockpit coaming.

It's difficult to imagine how a big sailing yacht could be made any better, because *Independence* represents the state of the art. But Fabio Perini is always thinking, and the next 18 years could be even more exciting than the last.

Specifications

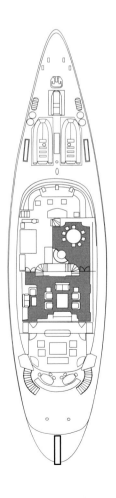

Value	Specification
53 m (173 ft 9 in.)	**LOA**
44.08 m (144 ft 7 in.)	**LWL**
11.41 m (37 ft 5 in.)	**Beam**
3.9 m (12 ft 6 in.)	**Draught (keel up)**
8.3 m (27 ft 2 in.)	**(keel down)**
562 tonnes	**Displacement**
1304 sq.m	**Sail area**
North Sails	**Sailmaker**
Perini Navi	**Masts**
Perini Navi	**Booms**
Perini Navi / Antal	**Winches**
2 x Deutz 1256 hp	**Engines**
2 x 125 kw, 1 x 80 kw Northern Lights	**Generators**
43,000 L	**Fuel**
Steel hull, aluminium superstructure	**Construction**
ABS Maltese Cross A1, AMS, ABCU, MCA	**Classification**
Perini Navi	**Naval architects**
Perini Navi SpA, 1998	**Builder/Year**

Spada

'Steel-true and blade-straight'

Robert Louis Stevenson wrote these words about his wife, who must have been quite a formidable figure, although the rest of his tribute to her is couched in more romantic terms. But he might have felt the same about the motor yacht Spada, had he lived another 100 years or so. For Spada is Italian for sword — there are several ceremonial swords aboard — and the vessel's hull was built of steel in Holland. She is true to the vision of her owner, whose extensive yachting experience was brought to bear upon the project. And she is straight, in an honest and seaman-like sense, for there is nothing quirky or ephemeral about her.

The owner's involvement with Dutch yachts is long-standing, and includes the pretty 23 m *Sirdar*, designed by G de Vries Lentsch Jr, and built at Amsterdam Shipyard during 1965. She made her way from Holland to New Zealand shortly after her launch, and has been a familiar and much-admired feature of Auckland's home fleet ever since. And so it was to Willem de Vries Lentsch that the owner turned, following a lengthy period during which he had written the specifications for the new motor yacht he had in mind. An introduction to Ken Freivokh by a mutual friend resulted in a contract for the interior design of the new vessel, which would be built at Hakvoort's Monnickendam premises during 1998.

Spada's lines are clean and traditional with a pleasing sheer that extends from her powerful bow to the point of her canoe stern. The treatment of her aluminium superstructure and the styling of her large windows are in keeping with her Dutch look, which is well founded and enduring. She is her owner's yacht in many respects, and he is a forthright individual whose qualifications include a Master's ticket earned during naval service. So it is no surprise that *Spada* has emerged as a handsome, ocean-going motor yacht that would inspire even the most timid mariner with a healthy measure of confidence.

Like *Sirdar*, *Spada* left Holland for New Zealand shortly after her launching, for her owner had an interest in the America's Cup. She took 11 months to make the trip, which began during November 1998 in the wintry waters of the North Sea. Tracking south-west towards Finisterre and the Bay of Biscay, she stopped in Gibraltar before making for Malta. Now enjoying some warmer weather, *Spada* sailed for Suez and the Red Sea, before Captain Christain Mehlmann set a course for Thailand via the Maldives. She broke her journey again in Singapore, the Whitsundays and New Caledonia, reaching Auckland on 2 October 1999, just over two weeks before the start of Round Robin racing for the Louis Vuitton Cup.

You can board *Spada* by means of the gangway, which stows in the starboard rail, or the passerelle, which leads from the dock to an opening in the bulwark at the tip of the stern. The after main deck is a pleasant, shaded area where guests can relax on two settees, which follow the contours of the varnished cap rail. A teak table, divided into three sections, is situated between the settees, and four steamer chairs are normally arranged on the forward side so that up to 10 can dine in comfort. A window to starboard of the double glazed doors leading into the saloon may be lowered so that refreshments can be served directly from the bar inside.

The saloon itself is warm and welcoming, with teak panelling complemented here and there by briar oak, some large, comfortable sofas and armchairs, and a bar ringed by several seats. Further forward, and to starboard is an attractive chess table, while the owner's desk is built into the corner underneath the foremost window to port. Curtains and carpets are in understated shades of raw silk and wool respectively, and the off-white headlining enhances the impression of space, which seems much greater than that normally found aboard a 34 m motor yacht.

Looking forward, you will see the central lobby through glass doors that are configured to resemble a bay window. The doors curve into the saloon between the bookshelves on the forward bulkheads, so that the lobby is almost circular in plan. Stairs spiral down to the guest accommodation, and up to the bridge and sky lounge. There are exits to the side decks to port and starboard, and a day head, which serves the saloon. A display cabinet contains the owner's collection of Royal Doulton ships' figureheads, and

One of the owner's collection of swords from which *Spada* takes her name.

in the middle of the stairwell stands *Sirdar*'s original upper deck telegraph, burnished to a degree that would gladden any naval officer's heart!

Moving forward again is the owner's suite and a further example of Ken Freivokh's spatial thinking. For the passage between the study and the stateroom wanders off to the left, skirting the bathroom to starboard and the crew lobby and galley which is the far side of a concealed door to port. In addition to creating a little mystery, this touch, like many others throughout the vessel, help to give the impression that *Spada* is much bigger than she really is.

The intimate study is furnished with a leather-topped desk and three chairs along with a glass-fronted cabinet containing books. The stateroom is generously proportioned being situated at the forward extremity of the superstructure on the main deck. This means that the owner enjoys a panoramic view over the foredeck and to either side through deep windows. The quality teak fitted furniture is accented with briar oak around the centrally sited, king-sized bed and on the small chests of drawers to either side. Stainless steel fittings predominate here, and throughout the accommodation, and they provide a cool contrast to the warmth of the teak and the oak. The bathroom features a large tub as well as a substantial, glass-fronted shower stall.

Moving back through the owner's suite to the central lobby, you take the stairs down

Spada's comprehensively equipped and well-appointed bridge.

Spada

to the guest quarters, which are arranged amidships between the aft engine room, and the crew mess and cabins further forward. There are twin staterooms to port and starboard, which benefit from the good natural light afforded by the large oblong portholes that are a feature of the lower deck. Each has an adjacent head and shower, and both are decorated in a style consistent with that found throughout the yacht. Framed antique charts of Mediterranean islands provide the visitor with clues as to where *Spada* has already been, and where her cruising itinerary may take her when she revisits the northern hemisphere. Further aft again is the VIP guest suite, which occupies the full beam of the vessel. A double bed is situated to port, while a desk is built into the after bulkhead opposite the entrance. The bathroom, which is similar to the owner's, has a shower as well as a generous tub, where a Very Important Person could comfortably relax with a drink before changing for dinner.

Because the owner's accommodation is situated forward on the main deck, where motor yachts of similar character sometimes have a dining room, guests are normally bidden to eat in the upper deck saloon, or sky lounge. Here you will find a dining table, a corner bar to starboard, and the predominantly blue and yellow fabrics that are a feature elsewhere in the yacht, as are the flowing lines of the fitted furniture. A dumb waiter is concealed in the forward bulkhead to port, above the galley. As in the main saloon below,

double doors open onto an after deck where the tenders are stowed when *Spada* is at sea. The Nautica and Novurania rigid inflatables can be lowered into the water by two custom-made Ascon cranes, which are located next to the guardrails on either side. While you can dine 'al fresco' with the tenders aboard, larger numbers of guests can enjoy drinks and dinner from the barbecue once they have been removed. Again, you are reminded of the extent of Spada's capacity for entertainment, which the owner specified when drawing up his requirements for the ideal yacht. He wanted her to be able to accommodate large, informal groups for parties, as well as providing suitable surroundings for groups of business associates to meet. *Spada* does all of these things, and is also perfectly suited for more decorous occasions as well.

Moving forward through the lobby, past signal flag boxes and bookshelves, you arrive on the bridge. Standing by the wheel, and looking over the superstructure to the foredeck, and beyond, you feel that this yacht could take you anywhere. Ahead, and to either side of you is a comprehensive range of instruments. The engine controls are duplicated on either bridge wing as well as to each side of the upper deck aft and on the flying bridge. These include joysticks for the bow and stern thrusters, which afford excellent manoeuvrability while docking. Three Recaro seats are arranged behind the instrument panel, with the central one mounted on flush-fitting rails so that the captain can swivel around to work at the chart table which is built into the after bulkhead. The Inmarsat communications system and security camera monitors are situated in the port after corner, next to the steps that you take to the flying bridge. A further staircase forward leads down to the crew lobby on the port side of the main deck, next to the galley. The bridge is panelled and furnished in teak, with white headlining.

An octagonal skylight is the main feature of the top deck, and this provides daylight for the stairwell below as well as giving a lofty air to the central atrium. Two captain's chairs sit forward of this skylight, facing the upper control and instrument panel, which is built into the leading edge of the flying bridge. A forward-sloping windscreen runs around the top

of this coaming, and this has the greenish tint that is a feature of the windows throughout the yacht. Guests have plenty of room for sunbathing around the raked mast, which also supports the Inmarsat dome, radar scanners, searchlights and foghorns.

Spada's deck layout allows you to move easily around the yacht, and taking the two flights of steps on the port quarter, you soon arrive back on the main deck. Heading towards the foredeck, you will pass the entrance to the engine room, and in these pristine, white surroundings you will find the two, 482 hp Caterpillar 3406E diesels that propel the vessel. These have the latest engine management system from the Illinois manufacturer and also boast soot trap and regeneration technology, which boosts exhaust gas temperatures to over 900°C. This means less pollution, and no soot on the hull. The yacht's design and technical specifications are of a very high order throughout, and comply with the strict letter of the MCA code. These regulations specify top-end firefighting and sprinkler systems, fire and waterproof bulkheads and doors, a comprehensive range of life-saving devices, GMDSS provision, and a multitude of escape hatches.

Back on deck, and passing by the galley, you may want to stop by and see what goes on. White work surfaces surround sinks trimmed in blue, and cupboards are finished in teak. The cook enjoys a good view through the large windows to port, which can be opened for ventilation or a draught of sea air. The stairs just outside the galley lead down to the crew mess and accommodation for seven, which is situated on the lower deck, forward of the guest quarters. A comfortable, U-shaped settee is arranged around a table to port, across the central passage from a small range with a sink to one side. A fridge is situated below this surface, and a television above. A triple cabin, along with a twin and a double, make up the remainder of this area, which is relatively roomy, as *Spada* sails with a complement of five. The ship's laundry is to be found in the forepeak, as is space for further storage.

The foredeck is home to twin Ascon windlasses, which handle lengths of chain that comfortably exceed Lloyds' requirements. Two 315 kg Poole anchors complete the inventory of ground tackle. Steel fender racks are fitted next to the bulwarks on either side, and an impressive ship's bell, mounted on a stainless tripod, enjoys pride of place amidships. A raised, teak-capped rail runs back along the gunwales from the jackstaff, providing additional security for those working on the bow.

Strength and seaworthiness are evident throughout the yacht, and there is a lasting quality to the furniture and fittings which transcends fashion. While she is new, *Spada* has already assumed the character of an older vessel, which is due in part to the owner's extensive collection of maritime artwork and naval memorabilia, some of which adorned his previous yachts. *Spada* will look as good in 50 years' time as she did when she left the Hakvoort Shipyard in 1998. And she will cover many thousands of nautical miles between now and then.

Specifications

Value	Specification
33.7 m (110 ft 6 in.)	LOA
7.92 m (26 ft)	Beam
2.6 m (8 ft 6 in.)	Draught
11.5 knots	Speed (maximum)
10 knots	(cruise)
2 x Caterpillar 3406E 354 kw (482 bhp) @ 1800 rpm	Engines
2 x 80 kw, 1 x 55 kw Northern Lights	Generators
Vosper Thornycroft	Stabilisers
59,220 L	Fuel
5500 n.m. @ 10 knots	Range
High tensile steel and aluminium	Construction
Lloyd's + 100A1, MCA	Classification
Willem de Vries Lentsch	Naval architect
Ken Freivokh Design	Interior design
Hakvoort Shipyard BV, 1998	Builder/Year

Spada

Affinity

Verde, que te quiero verde
(Green, how I love you green)

Federico Garcia Lorca had a thing about green, and it came through fairly strongly in his Romance sonambulo, written 1924–27. People feel differently about green, it arouses superstition in some while others like its fresh and verdant hues. You don't see many green super yachts, but when you do, you look again, for this is something exceptional. But the motor yacht Affinity would draw attention to herself whatever the colour of her hull, it just so happens that she is green, and it was that which caught your eye in the first place.

She stood out against the super yacht fleet in the Hauraki Gulf during the America's Cup series for many reasons, not the least of which was the purposeful line of her hull. This was drawn by Jay Miner of the Delta Design Group, optimised by Ron Holland, and built of fibreglass by Delta Marine Industries of Seattle.

ABOVE

John and Adrienne
Thomson's *Affinity* on the
Waitemata Harbour.

BELOW

An example of the superb
joinery aboard *Affinity*.

The gunwales on top of her bold bow curve inwards and aft to a break in her sheer behind the full-width owner's quarters below the bridge. The bulwarks then run true to the after extremity of her superstructure before taking another step down to envelop the lower fishing cockpit. Her upper profile is uncluttered and finished in brilliant white. The long run of her boat deck also serves as a helicopter platform, and can accommodate a Jet Ranger or single Squirrel. Her flying bridge is normally shaded by a white bimini top, and this is secured aft by the span that supports her mast, radar and communications domes.

John and Adrienne Thomson are seasoned sailors, and have owned a succession of racing yachts called *Infinity*. They had decided to build a mother ship for their global racing campaigns, which would be capable of long periods of self-sufficiency. They wanted a stable yacht with modest draught, which would enable them to dive in shoal waters. For fishing, they needed a separate cockpit with an integral bait tank. The yacht should also be able to accommodate large gatherings of family, friends, and guests. As experienced seafarers, they had determined that composite construction best suited their needs. They approached Jack Jones, co-owner of Delta Marine, who would oversee the build with project manager David Darwent.

Delta Marine has been building boats for more than 30 years, and is the industry leader in the construction of fibreglass super yachts. *Affinity* would measure 46.2 m overall, which is well into aluminium, if not steel, boat building territory. But composite construction is on the move, and offers numerous advantages, including ease of maintenance. Contracts were signed in November 1997, with completion scheduled to allow the new yacht to sail for New Zealand for the thirtieth America's Cup defence. It was a tall order, but Delta would launch *Affinity* during August 1999 and, following satisfactory sea trials, she would stop only in Honolulu and Papeete before arriving in Auckland.

A passerelle extends from a slot in *Affinity*'s starboard quarter, and this takes you over the swimming platform into the fishing cockpit. Here you will find the glass-fronted bait tank built into the forward bulkhead. The lazarette is below you, and items of diving and fishing equipment can be passed up through the central hatch in the fibreglass deck. Forward of the lazarette, beneath the main cockpit, is a small gymnasium to port, and the control room to starboard, and these can be reached through a door by the starboard stairway leading down from the fishing cockpit. The main cockpit sits in the shade of the helicopter pad at the after end of the boat deck. A broad, striped settee describes a shallow U within the after cockpit coaming, and two tables with several wooden chairs can accommodate large outdoor dinner parties.

Adrienne Thomson had told Scott Cole of Ardeo Design that she and her husband preferred 'a nautical look' for the interior. The pale fabrics of the saloon enhance the quality of the cherry furniture, and the character of the New England antiques. A fireplace with a granite surround with malachite and tiger's eye detail occupies the port after corner of the saloon. A painting above it conceals a plasma screen television. This offers several viewing options, including one through the lens of the underwater camera built into the bow bulb. By the fireplace is a round table and chairs. The handsome maple bar is situated aft, and to starboard. L-shaped sofas are arranged below the large windows to each side of the saloon, with a table to starboard, a sea chest to port, and easy chairs which can be swiveled in the direction of the television. A wooden peninsula marks the forward extremity of the saloon to port, and this is topped at its inboard end by a spruce pillar.

Beyond the pillar is the dining room, furnished in the same style of unadorned elegance as the saloon. Moving forward, and to starboard, you enter a maple-floored lobby, passing the stairs to your right, and a door to the galley on your left, on the way to the owner's quarters which comprises a study to starboard, with a full-width stateroom and bathroom beyond. Entering the study through glass-panelled French doors you find another example of superb joinery in the shape of the desk, which is made of cherry with burl veneer and inlaid wenge. To your right is a sofa and, above this, a concealed media centre. The desk faces outward, and the occupant can enjoy an ever-changing seascape while working.

The stateroom has windows to either side with a king-sized bed amidships, between two cabinets. These, like the bed base, are finished with the ropework trim featured elsewhere. A tallboy stands against the after bulkhead, concealing a television with bookshelves on each side. A sofa is situated to starboard between the corner bookshelf unit forward, and the chest of drawers, which adjoins the after bulkhead next to the door.

The master bathroom has a striking mural by Lynne Fensterer depicting colourful signal flags against a windy sky and a stormy sea. This extends across the forward bulkhead between the mirrors above the basins to either side. The central jacuzzi is finished in Spanish pink marble, as are the basin tops. The ropework theme is continued with tiny pieces of jade, which follow the perimeter of these surfaces. A glass-fronted shower compartment occupies the starboard end of the bathroom, with further storage space over to port.

The galley is divided longitudinally, with cooking range and ovens to starboard, and dishwasher, sink and coffee maker across the peninsula to port. Fridge and freezer cabinets are built into the forward bulkhead, next to the stairway leading down to the crew mess, cabins and laundry. *Affinity* sails with a complement of seven or eight, but there is additional room for racing sailors to dine in the crew mess.

The guest accommodation consists of four equally proportioned

The corner bar in the sky lounge.

Affinity

staterooms, each with adjoining head, shower and tub. Two have twin berths and pullmans, one a king-sized berth that can be divided, and the fourth has a queen-sized bed with a convertible sofa. Off-white fabrics serve to accent the cheerful cushion covers and the cherry furniture, and the quarters feature many pictures and models of yachts. Mindful of the cache of gems to be found aboard *Affinity*, you will be pleased to note that each stateroom has stones of its own. These include tiger's eye, red jasper, lapis lazuli and green aventurine.

Back in the lobby, you take the stairway to the boat deck, passing the door to Captain Mark Howard's double cabin as you make for the bridge. This business-like area is finished in neutral grey, accented with chrome, and two darker grey captain's chairs are mounted on pedestals to either side of the wheel. A central control bank is topped with five screens, which display radar and chart information, along with a comprehensive overview of the ship's systems. The chart table is to port of the console, and the captain's desk is situated aft of the door to the bridge wing on the same side. Raised seating along the after bulkhead takes advantage of the view through the raked bridge windows. An external control station is mounted on either bridge wing, just forward of the

stairways down to the main deck. Aft of the captain's quarters is the sky lounge. The maple floor is partly covered by a blue-bordered rug, with multi-coloured, circular patterns. The sofa and chairs are upholstered in pastel colours with Art Deco detail, carried through to the maple furniture.

The extensive boat deck aft carries two of *Affinity*'s fleet of four tenders including the 9 m *Pursuit* which is designed for diving operations. It has been reinforced for use as a helicopter pad, and recessed lighting enables pilots to land safely at night. A retractable control station allows the captain to dock the vessel from the boat deck, which is also used as a spectator platform for regattas. You can reach the flying bridge by way of the stairs by the sky lounge door, and you will emerge next to the spa pool underneath the mast assembly. The central part of the flying bridge is designed for relaxing, with reclining chairs between the pool and bar. Two captain's chairs address the forward control station between the U-shaped settees, which are built into the bridge coaming to either side.

That *Affinity* made it to Auckland on time was a major feat. But there is nothing about her to suggest that her builders had a deadline to meet. Her owners wanted a functional, low-maintenance yacht. Outside, there are no teak decks to scrub, and hardly any brightwork to varnish. Inside, liberal use has been made of Corian and fibreglass in the guest bathrooms. And while the yacht is no less comfortable for this, she is certainly not, in Adrienne Thomson's words, 'dark and overdone'.

Affinity will roam the Pacific and South-east Asia for the foreseeable future, possibly returning to New Zealand for the next America's Cup. So look out for the big green hull among the white boats. As it says in the Delta Marine brochure, 'What you'll discover may change the way you look at yachts. Forever.'

Specifications

46.2 m (151 ft 6 in.)	**LOA**
41.2 m (135 ft 2 in.)	**LWL**
9.4 m (30 ft 10 in.)	**Beam**
2.4 m (7 ft 10 in.)	**Draught**
345 long tons	**Displacement**
16.5 knots	**Speed (maximum)**
13 knots	**(cruise)**
2 x Caterpillar 3508B, 1000 bhp each	**Engines**
2 x 99 kw Northern Lights	**Generators**
Naiad 510	**Stabilisers**
70,300 L	**Fuel**
Fibreglass	**Construction**
Delta Design Group	**Naval architects**
Ardeo Design / Owners	**Interior design**
Delta Marine Industries, 1999	**Builder/Year**

Affinity

Georgia

An old sweet song

'Georgia, Georgia, no peace I find,
Just an old sweet song keeps Georgia on my mind.'

STUART GORRELL (1930).

Stuart Gorrell wrote these words to music by Hoagy Carmichael in 1930, but others were to have Georgia on their minds from September 1996 when Bill Sanderson offered them the task of creating the largest sloop-rigged sailing boat in the world for the American yachtsman John Williams. Bill had supervised the construction of Williams's previous vessel, Atlanta, at the Auckland yard of Alloy Yachts, and many of those involved with the build of that 36.9 m sloop would find themselves at the forefront of this new challenge.

Glade Johnson was one, and you begin to get some idea of the size of the undertaking from the design brief he received for the interior. This called for 'the highest level of traditional joinery, done in the classic style. High technology systems and entertainment facilities should be provided, but not seen.' It also stipulated that 'a formal dining room should be provided, as well as convertible dining areas in the lounge and cockpit'. Five luxury cabins were called for, as well as a small, dedicated gym, along with generous accommodation for a crew of eight. 'The vessel, in total, should be a no-compromise, state-of-the-art masterpiece for the twenty-first century.'

Glade had worked with Ed Dubois on the design of *Atlanta*, so he knew his client well. He would lead a triumvirate during the gestation of the 48.5 m *Georgia*, with Butch Dalrymple-Smith and Paolo Scanu bringing valuable experience to the project. Although Paolo Scanu comes from a sailing family, whose yachts included the 'J' Class cutter *Shamrock V*, much of his work as a naval architect has been with motor vessels. It was this experience that led him to propose an after engine room. But his background as a sailor was useful too, and his later comments give you some idea of the scale of the enterprise he was about to join. 'As motor yachts go, *Georgia* is not that large, but as a sailing yacht she is awesome, a daring accomplishment in technology and talent. To date, she is the largest sloop in the world with the tallest carbon fibre mast, the biggest sailing yacht built from aluminium anywhere, and the first large sailing yacht to be built to MCA regulations.'

Further priceless sailing knowledge was brought to the design team by New Zealander Godfrey Cray, whose extensive experience includes several Whitbread Round the World Race and America's Cup campaigns. Meanwhile, Tony Hambrook and his team at Alloy Yachts in the Auckland suburb of Henderson had arranged for the construction of another new building at the yard, and work on *Georgia* began during October 1997.

She was launched on 25 November 1999, and soon took her place among the yachts moored in Auckland's Viaduct Basin. For a while, she would lie alongside Dr Jim Clark's Royal Huisman sloop *Hyperion*, whose rig had been the tallest anywhere until *Georgia*'s 59 m spar had been stepped. She would shine in the company of some of the finest super yachts in the world, assembled to witness the Louis Vuitton Challenger Series and the America's Cup defence. And she would show off her speed on the Hauraki Gulf, taking part in the inaugural New Zealand Millennium Cup regatta the following February.

She made a wonderful sight during the races from Auckland to Kawau Island and back, from the set of her pristine North sails to the sheer of her powerful maroon hull. *Georgia* carries her superstructure well, thanks in part to the height of her masthead, but also to Glade Johnson's eye for line, as he has effectively disguised the loft of the flying bridge, and the depth of the enormous picture windows to either side of the saloon. There were many interested spectators, as well as participants in the event, and you might have shared the pride of her owner, and Captain Dan Jackson, along with all those involved in her creation, as New Zealand's sailing flagship took her place in the global fleet.

Finding *Georgia* on the waterfront is a little like locating the Sky Tower in Auckland, all you really have to do is look upwards. Having taken a bearing on her sky-scraping spar, the rest is easy, and you soon find yourself admiring the high gloss of her topsides. The colour of her hull is the same as that of her predecessor, *Atlanta*, and the deep red hue is a further characteristic that sets her apart from other super yachts, many of which are finished in white or blue. Standing at her stern, you look at the first of many masterpieces of engineering you will encounter throughout the yacht. The swimming platform, which folds out of the transom, also serves as a tender dock, while the telescoping passerelle has a reach of 3.5 m, and can be swung through 90 degrees so that guests can board from alongside as well as over the stern. Access to the lazarette and after tender stowage is through a large, hydraulically operated hatch in the stern bulkhead, which is revealed when the swimming platform is deployed. Steps lead up from both sides of this platform to the after deck.

Moving forward, you pass between two turned stainless steel posts, which form the entrance to the cockpit while supporting the after extremity of the flying bridge. The cockpit is completely covered by the upper deck, but is open to the sides, although folding screens can be employed to enclose it altogether if the air conditioning is to be switched on. There are tables to either side of the cockpit, each with settee and several chairs, and up to 16 can be accommodated for dinner. There is a barbecue just aft of this area to starboard, and counters forward and to each side are equipped with a refrigerator and icemaker respectively. Stairs to port of the saloon doors, next

Stairway to the owner's suite and after guest quarters.

to the engine room access, lead up to the flying bridge, and there is a day head across the cockpit to starboard.

You enter the saloon through pneumatically operated, curved stainless steel doors with fluted cherry wood columns inboard, and to either side. Two tables are situated to port, with a large sofa, divided by a fitted cabinet, forming the perimeter of the saloon on this side. Aft and to starboard is a granite-topped bar with four pedestal-mounted chairs finished in leather. Carpets and upholstery are a rich and varied mixture of greens and blues with beige and maroon accents, and the complex quality of the panelling is offset by the white, beamed deckhead with fabric inserts. Huge windows to either side offer an ever-changing panorama. At night, or whenever the blinds are drawn, you can concentrate on the 40 inch Mitsubishi television, which is built into a cherry cabinet on the forward bulkhead. This is one of seven similar systems installed aboard *Georgia*.

Forward and to starboard is the passageway through to the dining saloon, and the stairs down to the after guest accommodation and owner's quarters. The stairway curls to the left as you descend, past an alcove faced in pink and grey marble, and you emerge into a lobby with a mirror-fronted cupboard to port, and a pretty painting of a Mediterranean village to starboard. Moving aft through the arched doorway into the owner's stateroom, you are again struck by the exquisite detail of the joinery, from the raised and fielded panelling to the carved and moulded detail of the double bed to starboard. Here again, you will find fabric wall coverings and headlining. A central feature of the stateroom is the large cabinet, which conceals another plasma-screen television. This rises out of the furniture and can be directed to face the bed or the study to port. Touch controls on the bedside table allow you to adjust the lights or curtains before deciding whether to monitor the external video cameras, or choose from the video, audio, navigation or information channels. The study contains a leather-topped desk with chair and adjacent sofa, and features a sophisticated DVD and entertainment system by Sony. To starboard

Arched doorways are found in the guest quarters.

of the dressing table at the foot of the bed is the entrance to the owner's bathroom. Here, the twin basins, surrounded by marble, are flanked to starboard by the shower compartment, and to port by the separate head. The walls of the bathroom are panelled in cherry wood, with off-white inserts, and the floors are finished in marble.

There are two further staterooms off the lobby, along with a small gym next to the owner's quarters. These cabins are of similar size but the one to port has double and single berths while the other has a double berth and a sofa. The style of decoration is distinctly different, however, and this extends to the colour of the marble in the bathrooms, which varies throughout the yacht.

Climbing the stairs from the lobby, you take the passage along the starboard side to the dining room. On your way, you will notice some interesting old maps of the states of Louisiana and Georgia, which are framed and attached to the inner bulkhead, as well as a clock, specially built for the yacht. A door leads from this passage to the side deck, and a day head is located just beyond. This small cloakroom is decorated in black marble with a linear inlay, with fittings reflecting the Art Deco look you will have noticed in bathrooms around the yacht.

You have admired the cherry panelling, wenge detail, and the touches of bird's eye and burl elsewhere aboard *Georgia*, and the joinery in the dining room is a further credit to the craftsmen at Alloy Yachts. The inlaid dining table is situated athwartships, beneath a large crystal light fitting, and surrounded by 10 matching chairs.

Take the stairs at the starboard after end of the dining room, and you will reach the inside wheelhouse and captain's office. From here you can see forward through the bridge windows, while overlooking the dining room below. Captain Dan Jackson tends to drive the yacht from the flying bridge above, but all instruments and controls are duplicated here, including navigation and communications equipment. The captain's desk is situated to port, and there is a sofa built into the after bulkhead so spectators can observe the watch at work.

Back in the dining room, you take the spiral staircase down past the galley door to the lobby between the forward guest staterooms. These are configured in almost exactly the same way as the two cabins aft, but enjoy an atmosphere of their own thanks to the different fabrics and marbles employed. Having seen the television in the owner's stateroom, you may have wondered where to look in the other cabins. The big Mitsubishi screens are concealed behind mirrors over the chests of drawers built into the bulkheads. Storage is generous here, and throughout *Georgia*, and all cabins offer good

The quality of the joinery in this guest stateroom is reflected throughout the yacht.

Georgia

OPPOSITE

Georgia off the coast of New
Zealand's North Island.

OPPOSITE BELOW

A view from the saloon
through the cockpit to
the stern.

BELOW

Some of the best views can
be enjoyed from the seat in
the pulpit.

views through the patented Alloy Yachts portholes in the hull. Fresh air ducts are installed in each stateroom, while air conditioning and heating can be controlled independently in all areas.

Making your way up the stairs, you enter the comprehensively equipped galley through a door between two marble alcoves on the landing. Crew accommodation consists of three cabins with over and under bunks for two, and a double for the captain. A central corridor divides these quarters, which are arranged beyond the crew mess, forward of the galley.

You can reach the flying bridge from the cockpit or the inside wheelhouse. The twin steering stations at the forward end feature duplicate controls, and wheels made of laminated teak and holly with carbon fibre spokes. Behind the helmsmen are two teak-topped units containing a sink, glass storage, icemaker and fridge. The after end is furnished with coffee tables and settees to each side, and a spa pool amidships with room for eight. Beyond the pool, towards the stern, is a broad, upholstered area where you can soak up some sun after your spa. But putting pleasure aside for a moment, this is perhaps the best place to admire the vessel in its entirety.

Above you soars the mighty mast made by Southern Spars out of carbon fibre. The 515 sq.m mainsail, weighing 589 kg, is fully battened, and employs a lazy jack system on the 17.7 m boom. The five-spreader spar is supported with discontinuous rod rigging, which, at its base, is as thick as your wrist. The three foresails are furled by Reckmann units the size of a man. These sails, like the main, are made of carbon Spectra. The 1450

sq.m gennaker was built from 2.2 km of nylon sailcloth, and the total weight of the sails from the North loft in Auckland is 2100 kg. There are two Lewmar 111 winches on the foredeck for docking, and two more at the base of the mast for halyards. Two giant Lewmar 144 backwind drums handle the gennaker from the aft deck. The eight Alloy Yachts designed captive winches, built by Nilsen of Auckland, manage the blade, staysail, runners and guys, while further captives in the pump room serve the main sheet, main halyard, and boom preventer. The working sheet loads of 15 tons meant that not only did Alloy Yachts have to invent captive winches stronger than any others, they had to start by sourcing special rope and designing the winches accordingly. All is balanced by the 80 tons of poured lead in the shell keel, with a further 10 tons in the dagger board, and when *Georgia* is not sailing, she is propelled by a 1000 hp Caterpillar diesel.

Such statistics border on the incredible, but they are only part of the story of this formidable yacht. For she is the invention of a team that broke new ground at every stage of design and build, and she became what her owner asked Glade Johnson to create: 'a masterpiece for the twenty-first century'. Such is the super yacht market that there may be other, larger vessels in the future. But when people talk in years to come about the sailing yachts they saw at the turn of the century, they will, to paraphrase Stuart Gorrell, have *Georgia* on their minds.

Specifications

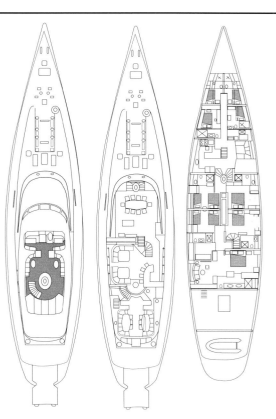

48.46 m (159 ft)	**LOA**
41 m (134 ft 6 in.)	**LWL**
10.10 m (33 ft 2 in.)	**Beam**
3.6 m (11 ft 10 in.)	**Draught (keel up)**
7.3 m (24 ft)	**(keel down)**
338 metric tonnes	**Displacement (half load)**
3473 sq.m (37,380 sq.ft)	**Sail area**
59 m (200 ft)	**Mast height**
Caterpillar 3508B, 1000 bhp	**Engine**
2 x 96 kw, 1 x 50 kw Northern Lights	**Generators**
40,000 L	**Fuel**
Aluminium	**Construction**
Butch Dalrymple-Smith, Paolo Scanu	**Naval architects**
Glade Johnson	**Styling/Interior design**
Alloy Yachts, 1999	**Builder/Year**

Georgia

Ilona

'Come, fly with me . . .'

One of the first things you notice about **Ilona** *is the blue and white Bell 407 helicopter perched aft of the mast on her sundeck. While it looks quite at home, it lends the yacht an air of imminent action, whether stern-to, at anchor, or under way. Her lines are purposeful too, with superstructure rising smoothly aft from a high bow before blending into three exterior levels amidships. Her profile is remarkable for the abundance of deep windows, an asset you will fully appreciate once aboard. And there is plenty of open deck space throughout, for the owners enjoy topside life as well as the comforts of* **Ilona***'s generous interior. For while she is a long-range, ocean-going yacht,* **Ilona** *also serves her owners as their northern hemisphere home, so she must be equally habitable in the colder climes of northern Europe as she would be in the Mediterranean, the Caribbean or the Pacific.*

The family's favourite tender is the 1964 Super Ariston Riva.

Her heritage is European, for Ed Dubois designed her to Det Norske Veritas scantlings, with a Redman Whitely interior. This London-based partnership had worked with Dubois to create the New Zealand built sloops *Sovereign* and *Kokomo*. The owners chose the fabrics and soft furnishings with Jenny Tudor-Miles of Beyond Design. While perhaps better known for his sailing yachts, Dubois had created the highly successful 50 m *Turquoise* during 1992, and was able to take the project over following the untimely death of Jack Hargrave, *Ilona*'s original architect. Pendennis Shipyard of Falmouth, England, won the order, but subcontracted the building of the hull to Bayard Aluminium Constructies in Holland to meet the stipulated delivery time. The hull would subsequently be shipped back to Falmouth and united with the superstructure that the English yard had completed. Like Ed Dubois, Pendennis had a solid reputation in the world of sailing super yachts with vessels such as *Adela*, *Mamamouchi*, *Taramber*, and *Wally B* to its credit. *Ilona* would be the yard's first motor yacht, and a pointer to the extensive capabilities of all involved.

Mike and Di Ebsworth were given the responsibility of supervising progress aboard *Ilona* prior to her launch in early 1999. Following a trip to London, where some photographs were taken against the backdrop of Tower Bridge, the yacht left for the Mediterranean, stopping in Jersey and Cadiz before reaching Gibraltar. Her owners were to enjoy the summer cruising in Italian, French, and Spanish waters, but *Ilona*'s programme included Sydney for the millennium celebrations, and Auckland for the America's Cup defence. Action was therefore imminent, and she would leave Barcelona for Valletta, Port Said and Djibouti, before making for Aden to reduce the risk of interception by the pirates that are sometimes encountered further down the African coast. Escaping this area unmolested, the yacht made for Bali, Singapore and Darwin, before arriving at her southern hemisphere home port to join the fun.

Boarding across the passerelle that spans the lower deck aft, you look down at the bathing platform and the entrance to the lazarette. The latter houses diving equipment, and provides access to the engine room. The main deck aft of the saloon offers plenty of room for dining or a cocktail party, and is protected from the wind by folding glass screens. The side decks at this level extend forward to the full width owners' suite below the bridge.

Entering the saloon, you are instantly aware of the fabulous views from the large windows. The pale fabrics and cotton wall coverings used throughout, and the cream-coloured deckheads, serve to accent the rich mahogany furniture, which brings warmth to these quarters, and to the dining room. Two cabinets frame the entrance to this area, the starboard one containing a bar and fridge, and the one to port disguising the audio-visual entertainment apparatus. The craftsmanship throughout is exquisite, and the stowage for cutlery and crockery in the sideboards deserves special attention. Nicholsons Yacht Interiors was responsible for the fitted furniture, while Hudson's of Worthing created free standing pieces such as the coffee and dining tables.

Moving forward on the main deck, you enter the main lobby to starboard. This provides access to the decks above and the guest accommodation below, thanks to the after engine room layout. The crew has a separate entrance to port. The lobby has a mahogany floor bordered with an inlay of dark wenge wood, and a chest at the foot of the staircase is faced with madrona briar, which is an occasional feature of the furniture around the yacht. Forward again, past a picture of the yacht's namesake, is the owners' suite. This consists of a study to starboard, fully equipped with telecommunications equipment and lined with bookshelves with an outward facing desk which allows the occupant to enjoy the view through two deep oblong windows of the type found throughout the owners' quarters. Two handsome oil paintings of sailing ships provide further scope for contemplation. Across the passage to port is a comprehensively appointed dressing room, with copious hanging space, wardrobes and drawers.

The owners' stateroom is decorated with peach and beige fabrics, with mahogany chests of drawers. There is a dressing table to port of the bed, and two sofas to starboard with an attractive camphor wood chest in between. A screen above the chest on the after bulkhead conceals a DVD player and television of the type found in the guest staterooms. The owners' bathroom features two heads, a steam shower with a teak seat, and twin basins, which are surrounded with black and gold Portoro marble, as is the bath. To refer to the Aqualux computerised jacuzzi in this way fails to do it justice, for the water that flows from the gold taps can be temperature controlled by means of a touch screen, as can the individual jets around the tub. This is arguably the most opulent space on the yacht.

The generously appointed lower deck accommodation has four double staterooms, another with an occasional double and a single berth, and a further single cabin equipped with a Pullman berth, which is used by the helicopter pilot. The after cabins are slightly bigger than the others, but every one has an adjacent shower room decorated with Verde Rajahstan marble. All six are named after the seas and oceans that surround the Australian continent, and each is accessed from a central corridor. Forward of the guest staterooms on the lower deck is the crew mess, and five cabins with over and under bunks.

Ascending via the lobby to the bridge deck, you will enter the wheelhouse through the

Ilona heads for the open ocean with her helicopter wrapped up.

captain's office to starboard. This area is comparatively austere, with a teak floor and a black leather settee across the after bulkhead from where guests can see Mike Ebsworth at work. Mahogany cupboards and drawers are topped with a surface largely covered with black leather and carbon fibre, with computer and radar screens arranged each side of the central console with its small steering wheel. Two captain's chairs are situated one to each side of the control panel, with a backrest for the helmsman placed amidships. The roof is finished in grey ultra-suede. Instruments include a Decca Bridgemaster radar, electronic chart systems, Anschutz automatic pilot, and a touch screen monitoring display for the ship's systems. An external Portuguese bridge, accessible from both sides of the wheelhouse, leads to the central stairway down to the foredeck. Aft and to port of the wheelhouse is the captain's cabin.

Making your way back through the office, you will reach the library. Mahogany bookshelves are in evidence, with comfortable sofas and easy chairs surrounding a coffee table to port. This table houses an LCD touch screen that controls the home cinema system. Select a DVD movie and the lights will fade, the blinds descend, along with a large screen to starboard, and a Sony digital projector will come down from the deckhead. Refreshments are also close at hand, for the dumb waiter can be summoned with goodies from the galley below. Should you be starting to feel a bit lethargic after the show, step through the after door, which leads from the library into the gym, with its Spirit running machine and Tectrix computerised exercise bike.

For fresh air, move aft again, and admire the range of tenders on the bridge deck. There are two Wave Riders stationed amidships, an 8 m, 12-passenger Nimbus diesel stern drive to port, and a classic 1964 Super Ariston Riva to starboard, which the owners bought in St Tropez. This varnished mahogany beauty, along with the other tenders, can be lowered into the water over retractable railings by means of a custom crane system incorporated in the deckhead. You are aware of an abundance of outdoor space aboard *Ilona*, and with the tenders over the side guests can gather for drinks at this level, or enjoy the privacy of the deck with a book from the library.

The view from the fly bridge will always be spectacular, whether at sea, in a pretty bay, or in the company of other large yachts whose decks you may admire from this perspective. But it is more than just a helipad: there is a helm station, bar with fridge and icemaker, dining area, barbecue (again served by the dumb waiter from the galley two floors below), as well as an Aquaspa six-seater whirlpool bath. This is situated below the mast assembly which arches over the top deck and supports both radar and satellite communications systems. There is also plenty of room for sunbathing, with comfortable sunbeds to either side of the whirlpool, and an abundance of reclining deck chairs.

Indeed the fly bridge may be the first place you set foot on the vessel, if you have flown in aboard the Bell 407. It may also be your point of departure when the time comes to leave. When you do, it will be with fond memories of a yacht that came to be as a result of the experience of her owners, who had 14 boats before commissioning this latest *Ilona*. The result is a yacht which is handsome and infinitely seaworthy, welcoming and supremely comfortable. Her interior is configured for both formal and family entertainment, and the atmosphere is that of home. Mike Ebsworth will tell you that many motor yachts become museum pieces before they are launched, for while they may be exquisitely adorned and ornamented, they have all the character of an expensive hotel.

We can look forward to seeing much more of *Ilona* in either hemisphere, whether fulfilling her duties as her owners' northern home, or coming back to Australia to be with them there. You will recognise her profile in any anchorage. Or you may spot the helicopter first.

Specifications

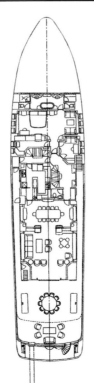
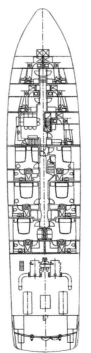

Value	Specification
45.6 m (149 ft 7 in.)	LOA
40.6 m (133 ft 3 in.)	LWL
9.5 m (31 ft 2 in.)	Beam
2.7 m (8 ft 10 in.)	Draught (half load)
340 tonnes	Displacement (light ship)
15.2 knots	Speed
2 x 960 hp Caterpillar 3508	Engines
80,000 L	Fuel
Aluminium	Construction
DNV	Classification
Dubois Naval Architects	Naval architects
Dubois Naval Architects	Exterior styling
Redman Whitely Design	Interior design
Pendennis Shipyard, 1999	Builder/Year

Ilona

Kokomo

The creation of a winning team

Alloy Yachts International was established in 1984, and launched its first super yacht Chanel in 1985. Over the next 15 years, the company added seven motor vessels, and 14 sailing yachts to the fleet, with the flagship, Georgia, being the largest aluminium sloop the world has ever seen. Ed Dubois designed five of these sailing yachts for the same owner, and all were built at Alloy's Henderson yard, west of Auckland. You will remember Esprit, Espada, Corinthian, and Sovereign, for they helped to establish Alloy's excellent reputation overseas, as did Imagine and Atlanta, also from the pen of Ed Dubois. And you will surely recognise the 40.4 m sloop Kokomo, for although she is more highly developed than her older sisters some family features remain, and her pedigree is unmistakable.

Whatever your business, it is always gratifying when a client comes back, and Alloy Yachts has attracted more than its share of repeat custom. But when an owner orders his fifth yacht by the same designer from the same yard, you know that the recipe is a good one. This doesn't mean that the team stops striving to improve the quality of the product; you only have to visit Alloy's Selwood Road headquarters to see the work in progress to realise that. For the 200 strong workforce that launched *Georgia* and *Kokomo* within 10 weeks of one another already has another three projects under way. Tony Hambrook's commitment to quality and innovation means that most components are manufactured in-house, and others are sourced from suppliers close by. Alloy's success has put it firmly in the lead of the burgeoning New Zealand super yacht industry, which is now the fifth largest by country in the world.

The three musketeers of Alexandre Dumas' novel were eventually joined by a fourth, and so it was with the creation of *Kokomo*. Redman Whitely Design had worked with Alloy Yachts before, most lately during the build of the 33.8 m *Charlatan*. But Justin Redman and Mark Whitely had also collaborated with all three during the building of *Corinthian* and *Sovereign*, so the alliance was already well established.

Kokomo was commissioned in late 1997, and the brief was to take the concept of mixing comfort, performance and elegant looks a stage further. This was made possible by somewhat increased length, greater draught, and a programme that included extensive

research into hull and keel design. Ed Dubois adds: 'We were working with a shipyard on what was to become the seventh construction to a Dubois design; a successful team therefore, and one where combined experience lent great confidence.'

Hull and keels were tank tested by Southampton University's Wolfson Unit (responsible for Team New Zealand's America's Cup research). The results included an easily driven hull, higher stability, with a keel and spade rudder which permit excellent manoeuvrability and good lift drag properties. Says Ed Dubois, 'This feature, combined with an easy tacking blade jib, allows this yacht greater tactical opportunities when sailing in fun regattas, an increasing feature of the large sailing yacht scene. *Kokomo*'s performance

ABOVE

The bright and informal
atmosphere of *Kokomo*'s
pilothouse.

under sail combined with her evident luxury has, we believe, taken the ideal of comfort and safety with speed significantly further.'

On the subject of fun regattas, *Kokomo*'s owner was adamant that his new yacht should be ready to compete in the New Zealand Millennium Cup, organised by Alloy Yachts' international marketing director, David Jenkin, and billed as the biggest race ever staged for super yachts. *Kokomo* fairly flew up to Kawau Island and back the following day, and had you not known that she had been launched only days before the mid-February event, you would never have guessed. *Kokomo*'s older sisters all have a dynamic look about them at sea, and the youngest member of the family would prove no exception, her flag blue

Kokomo will seem as striking in 20 years' time as she did when you first saw her.

hull surging through the swell under the spread of her spotless North sails. Even at rest, these big Dubois sloops look fast, for there is something about the curve of the coachroof and the set of the superstructure that suggests performance.

Stepping aboard the yacht, either via the bathing platform that folds out of the wide, reverse transom, or across the telescoping passerelle, you move into the cockpit between the after extremities of the coaming. Helm stations are situated to either side, and each has an instrument console, ahead of the wheel, with a full range of duplicated engine and sailing controls including the joysticks that manage the sail trim. Forward, and to either side are tables and settees, the latter upholstered in white with blue piping. This guest cockpit area can be shaded by a bimini top while the yacht is at anchor or under way.

You enter the pilothouse through forward sloping, pneumatically controlled, tinted glass doors. Visibility is excellent, and the yacht can be navigated from the captain's chair beside the indoor conning station at the forward extremity of this upper saloon to starboard. Radar and chart screens, along with wind instruments and automatic pilot controls, are concealed in a cabinet on this side, the upper surface of which hinges forward to expose its inner workings. Across the pilothouse to port is a comfortable sofa,

Kokomo's **powerful carbon fibre mast.**

with table and chairs, situated between the bar beside the steps down to the main saloon, and the stairway that leads to the guest accommodation aft. Redman Whitely Design developed the pilothouse as an area for relaxed conversation and casual dining, and the cherry furniture and babinga sole go well with the predominantly white upholstery.

There are many advantages to having the stairwell in the pilothouse. It allows two larger, half-width cabins for a total of four, and shortens the distance from the cockpit to the guest quarters. The lower saloon and formal dining area are not subject to any disturbance from those moving to and from these staterooms. The interior design and decoration theme creates the calm and inviting atmosphere sought by the owner, with focal areas of contemporary light cherry panels set into fabric covered bulkheads. Furniture pieces, beautifully made by Alloy Yachts, are cherry with lightly detailed panelling, with a number of burr walnut cabinets complementing the lighter cherry.

The guest quarters are divided by a panelled lobby with a walnut cabinet built into the after bulkhead. The two forward staterooms are down a few more stairs, and are situated to either side of the vessel. Both feature generous double berths, with sofas adjacent to the entrance to the bathrooms, which have an air of Art Deco about them with white walls, black marble surfaces, and judicious measures of chrome. Neutral beige carpets enhance the bright hues of the upholstery, and the owner's pictures add a further dash of colour to the white fabric walls. Patented Alloy Yachts portholes, screened by electric blinds, afford plenty of natural light.

Another, similar stateroom occupies the space to starboard of the lobby, across from the entrance to the owner's quarters. These are reached through an office, which has a walnut desk, suede chair and sofa, and plenty of book shelving along with a plasma screen television and DVD system. The owner's stateroom features the white walls and overheads found in the other cabins, and the cherry furniture includes a dressing table with adjacent, fitted drawers, a bow fronted cupboard under the flush-fitting television screen on the forward bulkhead, and large cedar-lined wardrobes. Aft and to port is the entrance to the owner's bathroom, which features twin basins and a glass-fronted shower cabinet, with black marble trim similar to that found elsewhere in the guest accommodation.

Back in the pilothouse, you move forward and down to the lower saloon and dining area. There is a blue sofa surrounding the table to port, and guests can relax here, or in one of the armchairs with pre-dinner drinks from the bar. Across to starboard is an inlaid cherry dining table with 10 chairs finished in tan suede, which contrasts well with the darker blue carpet. Panelling throughout is in cherry, while a handsome walnut chest of drawers stands between the doors in the forward bulkhead.

The four steps on the other side of the starboard door take you down to the day head and on to the galley past the entrance to the engine room. This area also acts as an effective division between guest and crew quarters. The galley is comprehensively equipped with the latest in catering hardware, as well as a large under-floor freezer in addition to the fridge/freezer compartments in the after bulkhead. Forward of the galley lies the crew mess for the permanent complement of five, with the captain's quarters and two double cabins beyond, each with an adjoining head and shower.

Reaching the foredeck by way of the crew entrance, you find the covered anchor wells just aft of the two Reckmann furlers that control the foresails. These are noteworthy, and are something of an Alloy speciality. The two plough anchors pivot upwards and forwards over the bow through the pulpit, from where they can be released. Not only is this a neat engineering solution, but it also means that the flukes do not spoil the rake of the stem, a thoughtful and aesthetically pleasing touch. Looking back down the sweeping teak decks, you will notice a solitary Lewmar winch, used for warping. With the exception of two larger Lewmar drums aft of the cockpit, which are used to trim the gennaker, this is the only visible winch, the others being the latest version of Alloy's patent captive reel type, which are concealed throughout the yacht.

The absence of any hardware enhances the clean lines of the white superstructure, from the 'pickle fork' extensions either side of the tender stowage forward of the mast, past the wrap-around dark glass of the pilothouse windows, to the after reaches of the cockpit. While this look is familiar among the big Dubois sloops, it is no less attractive for that, and *Kokomo* will seem as striking in 20 years' time as she did when you first saw her.

The tall white mast was made from carbon fibre by Marten Spars of Auckland, as was the Leisure Furl boom. The lowest of the five sets of

The clean lines of the superstructure.

spreaders supports a security camera and searchlight, along with a SatCom dome, and Navtec rigging keeps it all pointing skywards. Incredibly, the mast was stepped on the day the yacht was launched, and she made her racing debut just over a week later, with a suit of sails from North's Auckland loft.

After such an auspicious start, it seemed natural for *Kokomo* to emulate her sisters, all of which have boosted the Alloy Yachts brand abroad. She would leave New Zealand during April 2000 for Hamilton Island and Darwin, from where Captain Wayne Avery would shape a course for the Mediterranean by way of the Maldives. She is the latest in a long line of distinguished yachts from the desk of Dubois, built in Henderson for the same owner. But she is unlikely to be the last from this talented troika, whose partnership has done so much for the super yacht industry in New Zealand, for, with the help of Redman Whitely Design, they go from strength to strength. 'All for one, and one for all' was the rallying call of Alexandre Dumas' musketeers. You could hardly have put it better.

Specifications

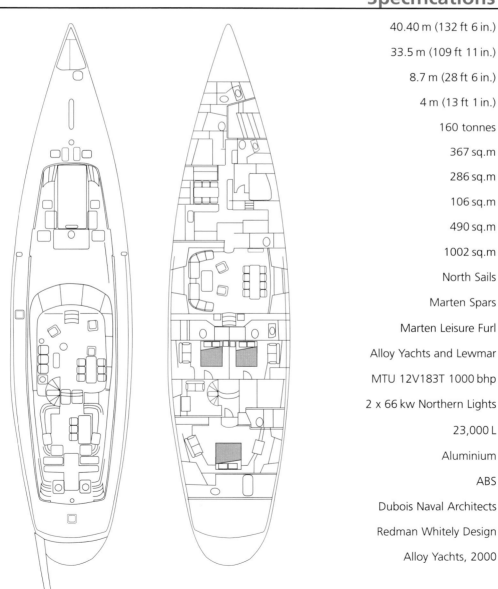

40.40 m (132 ft 6 in.)	**LOA**
33.5 m (109 ft 11 in.)	**LWL**
8.7 m (28 ft 6 in.)	**Beam**
4 m (13 ft 1 in.)	**Draught**
160 tonnes	**Displacement**
367 sq.m	**Sail area (main)**
286 sq.m	**(jib)**
106 sq.m	**(staysail)**
490 sq.m	**(reacher)**
1002 sq.m	**(gennaker)**
North Sails	**Sailmaker**
Marten Spars	**Mast**
Marten Leisure Furl	**Boom**
Alloy Yachts and Lewmar	**Winches**
MTU 12V183T 1000 bhp	**Engine**
2 x 66 kw Northern Lights	**Generators**
23,000 L	**Fuel**
Aluminium	**Construction**
ABS	**Classification**
Dubois Naval Architects	**Naval architect**
Redman Whitely Design	**Interior design**
Alloy Yachts, 2000	**Builder/Year**

Kokomo

Index

Bibliography

Bobrow, Jill, 1990, *Shenandoah*, Concepts Publishing Inc., Waitsfield.

Feversham, Lord, 1970, *Great Yachts*, Anthony Blond Limited, London.

Finger, Howard, 1994, *Double Haven*, Kingport Company Limited, Hong Kong.

Ketchum, Robert Glenn, 1996, *North West Passage*, Aperture Foundation Inc., New York.

Knox-Johnston, Robin, 1990, *Robin Knox-Johnston's History of Yachting*, Phaidon Press Limited, Oxford.

McCutchan, Philip, 1979, *Great Yachts*, Weidenfeld and Nicolson, London.

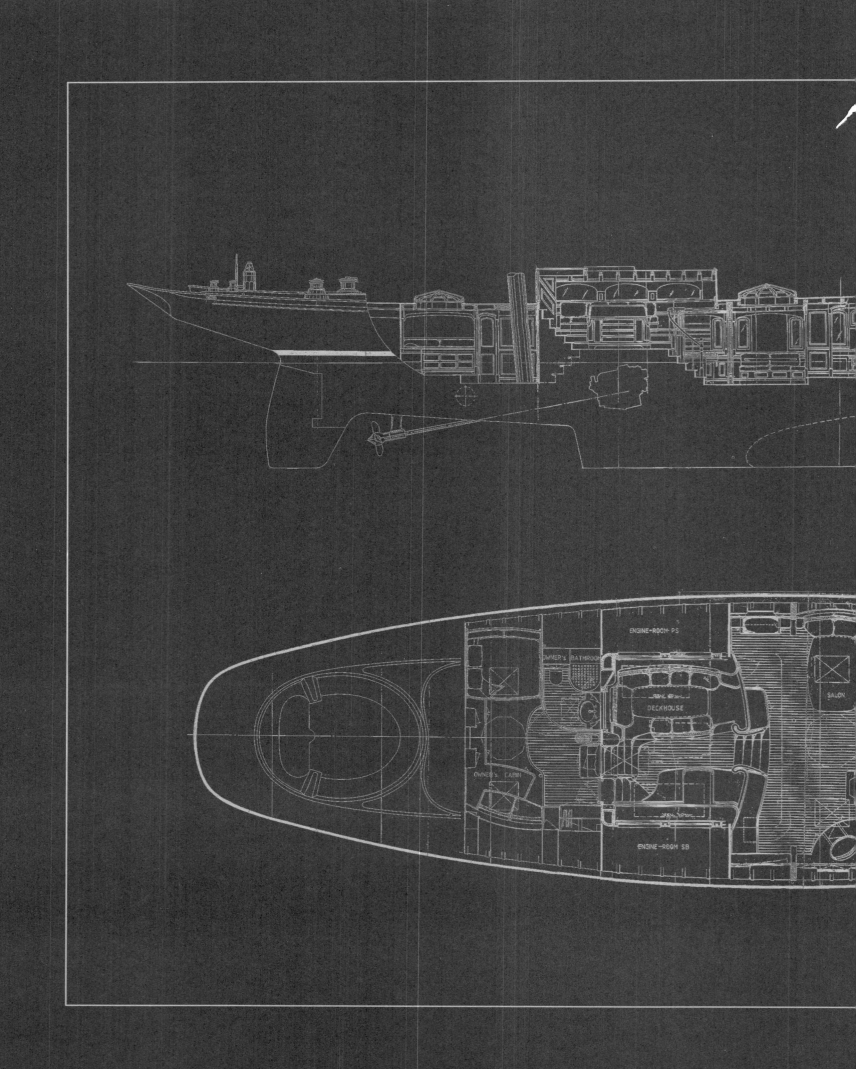